Spiders of the North Woods

Best Wishes!! :) !!

Spiders Are Cool :) :)

Spiders

of the North Woods

By Larry Weber

Larry A. Weber (signature)

Kollath-Stensaas
P U B L I S H I N G

Kollath+Stensaas Publishing
394 Lake Avenue South, Suite 406
Duluth, MN 55802
Office: 218.727.1731
Orders: 800.678.7006
info@kollathstensaas.com
www.kollathstensaas.com

SPIDERS *of the* NORTH WOODS

Printed in Korea by Doosan Corporation
10 9 8 7 6 5 4 3 2

Editorial Director: Mark Sparky Stensaas
Graphic Designer: Rick Kollath

ISBN-10: 0-9673793-4-2
ISBN-13: 978-0-9673793-4-0

Table of Contents

To Frannie,
who has been my companion in life
and has shared many wonderful moments
of spider watching.

And to E. B. White
who taught millions of children that
spiders can be loving and enjoyable critters.

Acknowledgements

Writing a guide to local or regional spiders has been a goal of mine for years. Though many good spider books have been published, they either deal with spiders from all of North America or emphasize the spectacular and well known ones (e.g. tarantulas) and do not show us what we are likely to see or observe near our homes.

I grew up being taught the same negative biases toward spiders as nearly all youth. But thanks to many people who helped me take a closer look, I saw that those frightful stories are exaggerated or simply inaccurate.

Thanks to my publishers, Mark Sparky Stensaas and Rick Kollath for seeing the value in such a book and allowing me to pursue it. Over the years, many others have helped me to learn more about spiders and see them more clearly. Allan Brady, William Shear and Fred Coyle all gave me a chance to learn more about spiders and how to recognize them. Larry West taught me how to see and photograph them. Bruce Cutler was very helpful in verifying spider species for me. Rhetta James, Dave Benson, Chris Evavold, Tom Diener and Judy Gibbs all gave me a chance to speak about spiders to their respective groups. As always, my wife Frannie was very supportive in this project and she corrected many a writing or computer problem for me.

And of course, I need to thank my students from The Marshall School of Duluth, Minnesota, who have often brought me spiders from their homes. Their enthusiasm is contagious.

Thanks to everyone, and I hope you will continue to enjoy spiders.
Larry Weber
October 31, 2002

Kollath-Stensaas Publishers wish to thank Larry for his full involvement in this major undertaking. His enthusiasm and knowledge of spiders is contagious. Both of us became enamored with the eight-legged ones.

Thanks to Dave Benson for proofreading the manuscript and finding those little mistakes that had eluded us.

Dr. Bruce Cutler of the University of Kansas helped us out with the identification of some tricky genera.

Though we mainly used Larry's splendid photographs and some of our own, we filled in the gaps with images from Larry West, Rod Planck and David Liebman–all fine naturalists in their own right.
The Publishers: Mark Sparky Stensaas, Rick Kollath
November 10, 2002

Why Should I be Interested in Spiders?

They live in our gardens, yards, fields, woods, wetlands and yes, even our homes. Populations of spiders are estimated to number in the millions per acre. They are invaluable predators in these habitats, each one feeding on hundreds of insects in its lifetime. Spiders are the creators of wonderful webs of several kinds. Like it or not, we all come into contact with these eight-legged critters and their webs many times during the year.

Yet, despite all of this, spiders–especially our local ones–are not very well known. Most of us are victims of sensationalist movies and magazine articles that dwell on the few arachnids possessing venom strong enough enough to hurt humans. Even spider books for children, tend to concentrate on the "dangerous" or poisonous ones. Most of the time these species live in other parts of the world. When we are told that almost none of our local spider fauna will, or even can, harm us, we are not likely to believe it.

Fortunately, many people are beginning to recognize the fact that most spiders are harmless, but they lack the training to distinguish those from the few that pose a threat to us. Often any black spider (with or without red spots) is suspected of being a black widow. And a brown spider in our house may automatically become a brown recluse. Indeed, when asked to name a few spiders, the response is often a short list including tarantula, black widow, brown recluse and daddy longlegs. The first three are not regular residents of the North Woods and the latter is not even a spider! Few would even think of the local jumping spiders, crab spiders, fishing spiders, wolf spiders or orbweavers.

Besides being harmless and valuable residents near our homes, spiders are just plain interesting. The construction of an orb web consisting of two kinds of thread, one sticky and one not, by a hunter that is virtually blind, is a true marvel. Each day the web is disassembled and the silk eaten. The spider can now recycle it into new silk to construct the next evening's web.

"Webless" spiders also reveal interesting behaviors as they hunt down prey. Often these spiders lay eggs in sacs that are protected and guarded by the mother. Two kinds will go so far as to carry their egg sacs around with them. The females of one family even allow the spiderlings to hitch a ride on mom's back for a few days. Young spiders use their newly formed silk glands to throw out threads that carry them off to new happy hunting grounds. "Ballooning," as this practice is known, has allowed spiders to colonize nearly every part of the world. Spiders are an extremely large and diverse group.

I invite you to step out beyond your own parlor to carefully observe, without any fear of harm, our fascinating neighbors. Even if we use cautious curiosity, we can get to know these eight-legged wonders of nature. Let *Spiders of the North Woods* help you along this path.

We tend to FEAR that which we do not KNOW

We tend to DISLIKE that which we FEAR

We tend to HURT that which we DISLIKE

but in the end

We tend to ENJOY that which we get to KNOW

What is a Spider?

Like other kinds of organisms, spiders have been classified into groups that further define them. All animals are put into large groups called phyla based on physical characteristics. Spiders belong to the largest phylum–the **arthropods**. Members of this group have segmented appendages and a hard outer skeleton (exoskeleton). This incredibly large phylum is basically composed of four major groups called classes: crustaceans (crabs, shrimp, crayfish, water fleas, etc.), myriapods (centipedes and millipedes), insects (flies, butterflies, bees, dragonflies, beetles, etc.) and arachnids (spiders, scorpions, ticks, etc.). Arachnids all possess eight legs.

This orb-weaving *Araneus* represents what we consider the typical , or "normal", spider.

Spiders are not alone in **class Arachnida**. Others sharing this classification include scorpions, whip scorpions, wind scorpions, pseudoscorpions, mites, ticks and daddy longlegs (harvestmen). Many of these critters are not found in the North Woods, but we do host several species of pseudoscorpions, ticks, mites and daddy longlegs. Spiders differ from other arachnids in various body features, even though all have the diagnostic eight legs.

Not a spider: **pseudoscorpion**

Within the **order Araneae**, all spiders are further divided into two suborders: **mygalimorphs** (orthognatha) and **araneomorphs** (labidognatha). Basically, the difference is how they use their fangs. The larger

Not a spider: **wood tick**

mygalimorphs inject the fangs downward into the prey. Included in this group are the tarantulas and the trap-door spiders. By strict definition and body features, they are not true spiders. There are no members of this suborder in the North Woods. The smaller and weaker araneomorphs clasp prey with fangs coming from the sides; a horizontal motion. Spiders in the North are all araneomorphs and are known as true spiders.

Not a spider: **harvestman; also known as daddy longlegs.**

Arthropod Summary

	Legs	Body Parts	Antennae	Wings	Gills/Trachea
Arachnids	8	2	0	0	Trachea
Insects	6	3	1 Pair	2 Pair	Gills/Trachea
Crustaceans	10 or more	2	2 Pair	0	Gills
Centipedes	Many *(1 pr./segment)*	1	1 Pair	0	Trachea
Millipedes	Many *(2 pr./segment)*	1	1 Pair	0	Trachea

This chart of Arthropods is a concise way of comparing the different groups. Take a look at how spiders differ from insects, a group with which they are often confused.

Insects superficially resemble spiders, but a closer look reveals many differences. Insects have three body parts; head, thorax and abdomen. Spiders have only two body parts. The head and the thorax are fused to form the cephalothorax, which is connected to the abdomen. Insects have three pairs of legs and two pairs of wings attached to the thorax. Spiders have no wings and four pairs of legs which are attached to the cephalothorax. Insects have antennae while spiders do not. Spiders, however, have another pair of appendages–the pedipalps–that are attached near the head. Insects have large compound eyes composed of many small lenses while the typical spider has eight simple eyes (rarely six).

Insect mouthparts are varied and complex and different from those of spiders. While many insects have biting or piercing mouthparts, they do not have fangs as found on the jaws (chelicerae) of spiders. Insects also lack poison glands.

Moving to the hind end of the body, many insects have stingers and/or ovipositors for laying eggs but lack the spinnerets and silk glands that spiders possess.

More differences between spiders and insects can be seen by looking at their life cycles. Insects go through a physically radical metamorphosis in which the young (larvae) change into adults that are completely different. Many also go through a non-motile pupal stage. Spiders do have an immature form that goes through several molts until adulthood is reached, but the young simply look like miniature adults.

While many insects feed as predators, many others are herbivores. All spiders are carnivores. Their animal prey may be quite diverse, but none are plant feeders.

Students of biology are taught the groups of classification from largest to smallest. These seven taxa are kingdom, phylum, class, order, family, genus and species. Each is a subdivision of the previous one and contains organisms with similar features. Such a scheme is far too simple, and taxonomy often involves the use of further divisions such as suborder, infraorder, superfamily, etc. When dealing with the spiders, species determination can be very difficult and is left to experts who can get a magnified view of the palps, jaws, epigynum, spinnerets, eyes and other tiny but diagnostic traits. This book concentrates on families and genera believed to be in the North Woods. Species are only identified if recognition is relatively simple.

Spider Parts: External Anatomy

Most of us are quick to recognize a spider when we see these specific features; eight legs and two body parts. Though frequently drawn incorrectly in cartoons, spiders have all eight legs attached to the front of these two body parts, the cephalothorax. The rear part of the body–the abdomen–is usually the larger of the two parts but has no legs attached.

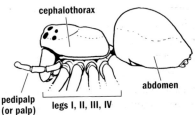

The **cephalothorax** is composed of a head region (cephalo) and a thoracic area (thorax). When viewed from above, the top, or dorsal, portion of this part is called the **carapace**. The underside, or ventral, is called the **sternum**. Usually, we see the spider's carapace, but with many web dwellers, the sternum can also be seen. Though the carapace is often without patterns or colors, many spiders have a central lower spot called the **thoracic furrow**. This longitudinal, depressed area is where the internal muscles of the sucking stomach are attached. Such powerful muscles are needed for its method of feeding.

Viewed from above (dorsum)

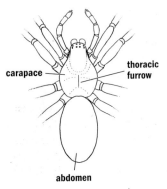

Viewed from below (venter)

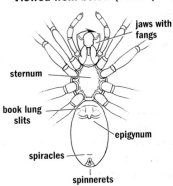

The cephalothorax has more than just legs attached to it. The **head**, as viewed from the front, has the same name as we use for the front of our head–the face. There are two main facial features; an **ocular region**–the area between the eyes–and the **chelicerae**, or jaws, located below the eyes. The vertical chelicerae are often lined with teeth and tipped with **fangs**. Venom is secreted from the fangs into the spider's prey.

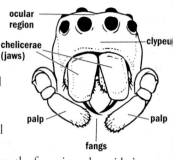

Slightly back and down from the face is a pair of appendages called the **pedipalps** (usually shortened to "**palps**"). In females the palps are merely segmented organs that look like miniature legs. But in males, the last segment is swollen and modified to serve as a semen receptacle for mating. They are fully developed only in mature males. Held out like little "boxing gloves", the male spiders are easy to discern with a little practice.

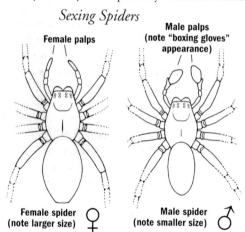

Sexing Spiders

Female palps

Male palps (note "boxing gloves" appearance)

Female spider (note larger size) ♀

Male spider (note smaller size) ♂

Ventrally (underneath) in front of the sternum is the spider's **mouth**. It consists of a simple opening that leads to the pharynx and stomach. Externally, the mouth has flattened structures called **endites** on each side and a **labium** (lip) behind.

Spiders are usually said to have **eight eyes**. Though this is the normal situation, eye numbers in species around the world can vary from eight to six to four to two...and even some with none. In our region all have eight eyes with two six-eyed exceptions, some members of the genera *Pholcus* (cellar spiders) and *Scytodes* (spitting spiders).

Eight-eyed spiders usually have their eyes arranged in two rows; an anterior row towards the front, below the ocular region, and a posterior row above or behind these. Eyes are grouped in pairs and named for their location. Those in the middle of the

front row are called **anterior median eyes (AME)** and those to their sides are the **anterior lateral eyes (ALE)**. Similarly, among the posterior eyes are the **posterior median eyes (PME)** and the **posterior lateral eyes (PLE)**.

[Diagram labels: posterior median eyes (PME), posterior lateral eyes (PLE), anterior lateral eyes (ALE), anterior median eyes (AME)]

In many spiders, all eight eyes are similar in size, shape and function; but exceptions are common. Often the rows of eyes are not straight but curve either towards (procurved) or away from (recurved) the front. Among jumping spiders, the posterior lateral eyes (PLE) are tiny and extremely recurved, often far back on the carapace.

Sedentary web hunters have poor eyesight, but active hunters often have large eyes with good sight. Most noticeable of these are the wolf spiders (Lycosidae) and jumping spiders (Salticidae). While wolf spiders have large posterior median eyes (PME), the jumpers have big anterior median eyes (AME). Wolf spiders are usually nocturnal hunters while the jumping spiders pounce on their prey in the daytime. This behavior and their mating habits (which we'll discuss later) seem to indicate that they can see color as well–an unusual ability among spiders.

This jumping spider has better vision than most spiders. Note the prominent anterior median eyes (AME).

Spider eyes and their arrangement vary enough that they can serve as means of identification. Just as we look at human faces for recognition, so too can we look at the face of a spider.

The abdomen is attached to the cephalothorax by a small tube called the **pedicel**. Usually much larger than the cephalothorax, the **abdomen** ranges from being just a long, thin organ to being very large and ball-shaped. Typically, the abdomen is oval when viewed from above. This is the part of the body most noticed in the field, and fortunately, it is often adorned with spots, bands or other patterns that help us identify the spider to genus or species.

Though no legs attach to the abdomen, it does have its own appendages. Connected to the undersides of the terminal end, but sometimes still visible from above, are the **spinnerets**. We can usually only see one pair in the field, but there are actually three pairs. Typically, the first and third pairs are the longest with the second pair being very small. Agile and flexible like fingers, spinnerets are used in ejecting and placing silk from the internal silk glands.

Also on the underside, next to the spinnerets, are several orifices of importance. Two transverse lines in the fore region are the slits that open to the internal breathing strata known as the **book lungs**. Also nearby are the genital openings. In females, this opening is often covered, or partially covered, by a structure called the **epigynum**. It is

The common grass spider — note the prominent spinnerets.

species-specific and connects with the male's palp tip, or **bulb**, in mating. The different epigynum forms are used by experts to determine spider species. Such an undertaking is difficult and demands the use of a microscope. Near the spinnerets are two other tiny openings, the **spiracles**–used for limited respiration–and the **anus**.

Some of the larger spiders appear to have indented depressions on the upper surface of their abdomen. These **dimples** are actually muscle attachment points from the inside of the exoskeleton.

While the cephalothorax in many spiders is devoid of hair and smooth and shiny, the abdomen of these same spiders is frequently covered with thick hairs. While most of the hairs are short and straight, some have impressive modifications. Among these are the abdominal hairs of female wolf spiders (Lycosidae). Since part of the spiderling's development is to ride on mom's back, the hairs are shaped with small knobs or "handles," making holding on a bit easier. Tarantulas have abdominal hairs modified to protect themselves. When threatened, tarantulas can brush off clouds of these hairs with their hind legs. Each hair is covered with tiny hooks and can cause severe itching when coming in contact with skin, especially around the nose and eyes.

For many people, no part of the spider's anatomy is more noticeable than the **legs**. Because of our stereotypes, we may assume that all spiders have very long, hairy and fast moving legs. But a closer look shows us that spider legs range from short to long, thick to thin, hairy to smooth, and though many spiders are fast moving, a large number are slow and don't move much at all.

Traditionally, spider length has been measured from the face to the spinnerets on the rear–basically, body length excluding the legs. Though this is a useful measurement, body length is not what most people think of when describing a spider. In this book, we also use the legspan to describe overall spider size. It is measured as the distance from the tip of the front legs to the tip of the hind legs.

Legs are consistently composed of seven segments, more than most other arthropods. Starting from the cephalothorax and going out, the

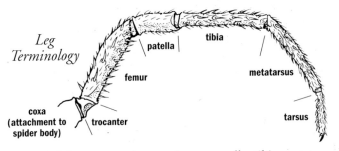

Leg Terminology

coxa (attachment to spider body) · trocanter · femur · patella · tibia · metatarsus · tarsus

parts are called the **coxa**, **trochanter**, **femur**, **patella**, **tibia**, **metatarsus** and **tarsus**. With the exception of the first two, the names are similar to those of human leg anatomy. At the far end of the tarsus, spiders possess **claws**. Depending on the species, there are either two or three claws. Web-making spiders and a few wandering hunters have three claws. The two-clawed spiders do not make webs but can be either active or sedentary hunters.

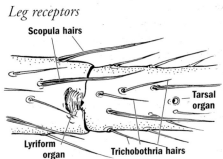

Leg receptors

A close-up view of a section of a spider's leg showing four kinds of receptors:

Scopula: simple tactile hairs

Trichobothria: hairs that react to air movement and low-frequency vibrations

Tarsal organs: pores that sense humidity or chemicals

Lyriform organs: a scaley patch that senses leg stress

Scopula hairs · Tarsal organ · Lyriform organ · Trichobothria hairs

Spider legs are usually covered with hairs, but these hairs can show quite a bit of structural variation. Most numerous are the simple, short hairs that serve a tactile function. Scattered among these hairs may be short, sharp **spines** and/or long, thin hairs called **trichobothria** which are especially sensitive to surrounding conditions. Thick tarsal hairs called **scopula** show up on some species. Members of one family, the cobweb spiders (Theridiidae), have thick bristles on the tarsus. Used to pull out silk to wrap over struggling prey, these "**combs**" lead to the other common name for this family–the comb-footed spiders. Many spiders also have tufts of hair among the claws at the end of the tarsus.

One unique group of spiders has another abdominal structure near the spinnerets called the cribellum. The **cribellum** spins a special silk called "**hackled band threads**". Such spiders also have a thick line of hairs, the **calamistrum**, on the metatarsus. The cribellate families in the North Woods include the Uloboridae (hackled orbweavers), Amaurobidae (hackledmesh weavers) and Dictynidae (meshweb weavers).

Types of spider claws

Claws of web-weaving spiders

upper claws

median claw

serrated bristles

Claws of active-hunting spiders

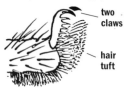

two claws

hair tuft

Spider Silk

The ability to spin silk and make webs are hallmarks of the spider. Indeed, the name spider originated from the word "spinder," in reference to its spinning ability. Spiders are arachnids and even this name comes from a spinning reference in Greek mythology. Arachnea was turned into a spider and forced to spin and weave for eternity because she dared to challenge the goddess Athena in this activity.

With only a few exceptions, all spiders have six spinnerets arranged in pairs at the posterior end of the body. Usually they are not visible, but in some families such as the Agelenidae (funnel weavers), they appear as twin tails. Each individual spinneret serves as a spigot to the internal silk glands. The complex silk material is formed as a liquid in the body, but upon being forced out and exposed to air, it quickly solidifies into the well-known threads, or silk, of the spiders.

Spinnerets can attach to six different types of silk glands. Different combinations of glands and spinnerets produce silk for seven different functions:

The buffet is ready! A shoreline web is loaded with many victims.

WEB CREATION: Both sticky and non-sticky threads are used to produce the hunting snare.

SWATHING PREY: Wrapping victims for immobilization and later consumption.

EGG SAC FORMATION: Creating the outer covering of the egg sac.

SPERM WEB CONSTRUCTION: The males make this tiny receptacle so they can fill their palp bulb with sperm.

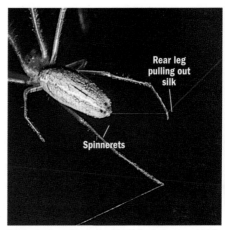

A *Tetragnatha* spider in the midst of spinning an orb web.

RETREAT BUILDING: Making a retreat out of silk or using silk to connect leaves to form a shelter.

DRAGLINE FORMATION: Making the ever-present dragline that many spiders constantly trail behind them or use to lower themselves from a height.

BALLOONING: Producing the silk that spiderlings use to disperse with the wind.

Spider silk is a most remarkable substance. Formed as a complex protein liquid within the glands, it quickly becomes an elastic solid thread when outside the body. Not only does silk have a tensile strength greater than bone or tendons per weight, but it is also so elastic that wet threads

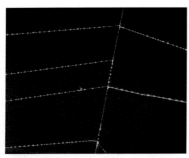

The spokes or radii of a web are non-sticky; allowing the spider to move around freely. But note the tiny packets of "glue" on the spiral.

can stretch to more than 300 percent of their length before breaking. The tenacity of spider silk is slightly less than that of nylon yet it is twice as elastic. Silk proteins are largely recovered by spiders from old webs and recycled for new ones. Before building a new web, the spider (especially, the orbweavers) eats the old one. Radioactive tagging has indicated that 80 to 90 percent of the initial web material shows up in the new web, even though it may be only a half hour between destruction and new construction. Apparently, the chemistry of silk allows for quick digestion and rebuilding.

Web Types & Construction

Virtually every spider uses silk in some capacity, but only the sedentary web hunters use it for snaring prey. Hunting webs are also known as hunting snares. Though sometimes a bit hard to define, web types are usually put into four categories.

1. IRREGULAR COBWEBS. A maze of threads randomly crisscrossing in no particular order. We usually notice cobwebs indoors or near buildings even though they are abundant in the natural landscape as well. In the North Woods, it is the members of the family Theridiidae (cobweb weavers), Pholcidae (cellar spiders), and Dictynidae (meshweb weavers) that make irregular cobwebs. Only the outer threads may be sticky, and then only on some webs. Spiders usually sit inverted in the center.

A frost-coated cobweb made by a member of the Theridiidae, the cobweb weavers.

2. SHEET WEBS. Threads anchor a platform or horizontal sheet in grass and bushes. The sheet may be flat, convex or concave. Webs can be complex and beautiful when coated with dew. The well-known Bowl & Doily Weaver webs and Filmy Dome Spider webs are elaborate examples of sheet webs. Most of the web is non-sticky and only tacky along the trapping threads above the sheet. The best known sheet web family in the North Woods is the Linyphiidae (sheetweb weavers), but variations of the sheet web or similar ones can also be seen in the Micryphantinae (dwarf spiders) and Hahniidae (hahnid spiders). Spiders often sit inverted beneath the sheet; pulling victims through the bottom of the flat web.

"Bowl & doily" sheet web.

Orb web construction

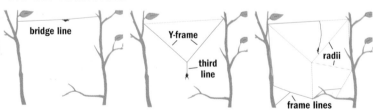

1. Spider "balloons" out silk. When silk gets snagged, spider tests the hold and then reinforces it with more lines.

2. Spider trails a loose second line, fixed at either end of the bridge line. A third line is made in the middle.

3. Spider returns to frame and spins outer anchoring threads and more radii (spokes).

3. FUNNEL WEBS. Sometimes considered to be a variation of the sheet web, funnel webs tend to be flatter and with a funnel-shaped opening in the center. Here the spider sits in retreat, waiting to dash quickly out and grasp tangled prey. The web threads are not sticky. The best known spiders to make this type of web are members of the family Agelenidae (funnel

weavers). We often see these webs indoors on windowsills, in corners, basements, under eaves and on outbuildings.

4. ORB WEBS. These are the familiar circular webs of the stereotypical spider. Even though three families in our region make these webs; Uloboridae (hackled orbweavers), Tetragnathidae (long-jawed orbweavers) and Araneidae (orbweavers), it is this last family that is most common-

Funnel web of the grass spider; family Agelenidae.

ly observed. Webs are usually vertical and many are high enough above the ground to be called aerial webs. Threads that anchor the web or extend to the center hub are called spokes (or radii) and are not sticky. Those connect-ing the spokes and spiraling to the hub are sticky. It is these viscid spirals that hold the prey. The web makers sit in the hub or off to the side. Some will even roll up a nearby leaf and use it as a retreat. Here they wait to feel the vibrations of prey caught in the snare. Eyesight of these orbweavers is so poor that most probably cannot see across their own web, and must rely on feeling alone to locate their catch. Orb webs are abundant in late summer. They may be large

The stereotypical spiderweb; the orb web.

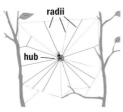

4. Once the frame and radii are completed, a tight, spi-ral hub is spun.

5. Next, a temporary spiral stabilizes the web and cre-ates "stepping stones" for spinning the sticky snare.

6. The spider now retraces its steps, eating the tempo-rary threads, and replacing them with sticky threads.

At sunset, this long-jawed orbweaver (Tetragnathidae) weaves its hunting snare in a marsh bordering a lake. The web should be loaded with flying insects by morning.

and beautiful, but the spider still needs to take them down and remake them each night, or at least every few days. Webs of the Uloboridae are rare in the North Woods and this strange family makes orb webs with no sticky threads.

Construction of the orb web always follows the same procedure (see illustration on pages 10-11. First a **bridge** is made. The spider shoots out a thread of sticky silk from its spinnerets. If it catches and the spider feels it catch, a bridge has been established. Next the spider reinforces it by walking back and forth on it, laying down more silk. A thread is fastened in the center of the last loose horizontal thread and the spider lowers itself down to attach this thread below. Tightening this vertical thread, the spider forms a **hub**. Climbing back up to the hub, and then to the sides, the spider forms a number of **radii** or **spokes**.

Spokes are at intervals that allow the spider to step from one to another. Small spiders tend to make webs with more spokes than larger spiders. Next a temporary spiral is made near the hub. Once completed, this is later taken up when the new, sticky and more numerous **spiral** threads are put in place. Sometimes the entire spiral is made up of a single thread; from the outer edge all the way to the center. Between the hub and spirals there is often a space with no spirals. This **free zone** may allow the

stabilimentum

hub

free zone

spider to step between the spokes and switch sides on this vertical web.

Construction of the entire web may take about one-half hour. About five minutes is needed to build the framework and radii. The sticky spiral section requires about twenty minutes.

Some spiders produce a zigzag formation in the hub called a **stabilimentum**. It is most common in the genus *Argiope*. The purpose of this structure has been a mystery, but recent research has shed some possible light on the topic. These special threads stand out in ultraviolet light possibly attracting insects who can see in UV light. It also may help to disguise the spider who sits right in the middle of the stabilimentum.

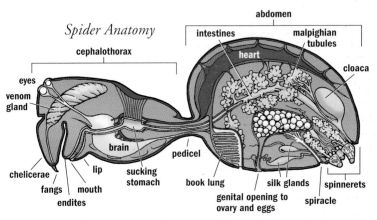

Spider Anatomy

The Inner Spider: Internal Anatomy

To most observers, the spider's internal anatomy is a mystery, but a look at the parts and their function can help us better understand their behavior. Spider insides vary little from species to species so let's take a look inside the cephalothorax and abdomen of a typical spider.

The nervous system (including brain and optic nerves), stomach and poison glands take up most of the cephalothorax. In the abdomen, we find the heart, midgut, malpighian tubules (primitive kidneys), ovaries, respiratory organs (book lungs and trachea) and the silk glands with tubes leading to the spinnerets. Since the abdomen contains so many vital organs, any damage to this part of the body can lead to a quick death for the spider.

Of special note in the cephalothorax is the **sucking stomach** and the poison glands. Spiders eat all meals in liquid form and so after catching prey and injecting it with venom to subdue it, they also must inject enough enzymes to liquefy the organs. They now have an insect milk shake right in its own ectoskeleton container. They suck up their meal through the mouth, down the pharynx and into the stomach. The powerful stomach muscles required for this activity are attached to the insides of the carapace–the site called the **thoracic furrow** (which is visible on the carapace). Larger spiders will use their legs and feet to crush the exoskeleton of their prey as they feed, while smaller ones leave the shell intact.

With the exception of the family Uloboridae (hackled orbweavers), all spiders in the North Woods possess **poison glands**. Tubes that open at a pore near the tip of the cheliceral fangs reach down from the glands above. Cylindrically shaped, these poison glands fill the space above the mouth, behind and below the eyes. The glands may extend back beyond the middle of the cephalothorax, but in some species they are so small that they hardly go beyond the base of the chelicerae. **Venom** produced by a spider may vary with their age and physical condition. Only a few species have venom virulent enough to be harmful to humans, and none regularly live in the North Woods. Remember, spiders are timid; and even if provoked to attack, most have fangs that are too tiny to puncture human skin.

Spider Biology 101

Eggs, Egg Sacs & Nursery Webs

Spiders produce eggs during the summer and females deposit these when they are fertilized, about one week after copulation. The number of eggs varies widely; a few species may produce only one or two eggs, some have 25 to 30, many form 100 to 300, and in one situation, more than 2500 eggs were counted in a single egg sac of an orb weaver. Most are about one millimeter in diameter. Groups of these tiny white balls are wrapped in silk by the female to form an **egg sac** (sometimes called a cocoon). Most sacs are spherical (though some may be other shapes) and five to ten millimeters in diameter.

A female Goldenrod Crab Spider attaches her egg sac to a folded leaf.

Many spiders attach this egg sac to the web, usually along the edge. A good example of this can be seen in the Theridiidae (cobweb weavers). Others hide the sac under bark, in a folded leaf or in another convenient hiding place. In many species the female will stand guard over the egg sac. Some species make more than one egg sac and occa-

Wolf spiders carry their egg sacs attached to the spinnerets.

sionally three or four may be seen in one web at the same time.

Spiders that typically construct silken **retreats** for their own hiding places will use these same sites to hide the egg sac. Standing guard over these sacs is such a full time commitment for some spiders, that they remain on duty until death.

Four families of spiders are noteworthy when it comes to the handling of their egg sacs. The Pholcidae (cellar spiders)

A Nursery Web Spider carrying her egg sac before placing it in the specially made nursery web. It is attached to both the spinnerets and her jaws.

The Pisauridae's (fishing spiders) egg sac is held by the female in her jaws, but with some threads from the spinnerets also attached. The sac is held more directly under the body than as in the cellar spiders or spitting spiders. Even in this awkward position she goes about her daily routine.

wrap the eggs in just a few thin threads. The actual eggs can be seen right through the scanty covering and it seems the mass will fall apart any second. Once formed, the egg sac is held in the female's jaws as she sits inverted in her irregular cobweb.

The Scytodidae (spitting spiders) carry their eggs too. The egg sac is held in the jaws of the female. She has no web to call home and so carries the sac with her wherever she goes.

Two genera of the Pisauridae (nursery web spiders) take this same style of egg-carrying and add a touch of their own. Egg sacs are held by the chelicerae (jaws) but with some threads from the spinnerets also attached. The sac is held more directly under the body than as in the cellar spiders or spitting spiders. Seemingly awkward, these spiders manage to move

Folded leaves secured with silk make a fine nursery web for the young Nursery Web spiderlings (*Pisaurina*).

about with the huge sac held under their body. No wonder most stay in hiding or limit their movement during this time. Egg-carrying appears to be most inconvenient for the fishing spiders (*Dolomedes*) since they are used to moving about on the surface of the water. Shoreline rock crevices provide safe retreats for females during this stage. A nursery web spider (*Pisaurina*) female will hold the egg sac in her jaws and spinnerets for a while but then place the sac on a plant leaf, such as a milkweed. She then binds the leaf around her eggs with silk forming an elaborate network of threads and creating a safe hiding place for the young called a **nursery web**. But just to be sure, the female will

stand guard. Usually these large brown-black spiders are seen waiting dutifully, face-down on the stem of the same plant that holds their egg sac.

Mama wolf spider pulls baby sitting duty as she carries around all her spiderlings. They cling to specially modified hairs on her back.

Spiderlings

Lycosidae (wolf spiders) are maybe the best known of any spiders when it comes to parental care. The female produces a large egg sac, usu-

ally just a bit smaller than the abdomen, and attaches her treasure to the spinnerets. She goes about her business for a couple weeks, wandering around with this white or brown bag on her tail end. (Overwintering adults can be seen with the sac already formed during May, but wolf spiders also produce egg sacs though most of the summer.) Her dedication as a mother does not end with the eggs,

Dozens of spiderlings inhabit the web of their mother until sibling-cannibalism makes it an inhospitable place to stay. Dispersal is the next step in life.

though, as she continues to provide transportation after they hatch. The young climb up on her abdomen and stay there for another week to ten days. She does not feed them. They live off their tiny yolk sacs. Since mother wolf spider often stays in hiding while she carries her family, we seldom see this fascinating spectacle of summer.

The tiny baby spiders, known as **spiderlings**, all hatch from the egg sac at the same time. Tiny and blind at first, they remain near the egg sac for a few days. Soon they **molt** through more advanced stages until they begin to resemble the adult spider in body shape and markings. Slowly, their eyes grow and they develop the ability to spin silk. Unable to feed at first, they subsist on an internal yolk sac.

Following the next molt, their fangs develop and they are now able to feed. They quickly learn that their own siblings make a tasty and convenient meal, so **cannibalism** becomes common. To cope with this new threat, the spiderlings start to move away from the family group and disperse. It is also at this time, especially among some of the Theridiidae (cobweb weavers), that a limited social behavior temporarily exists. Not only are the young allowed to stay on the web with the adults, but the females will regurgitate a liquid for the spiderlings to feed on. Of course, young wolf spiders tolerate each other as they ride around on mother's abdomen. True adult social spiders exist only in the tropics. All adult spiders in the North Woods are loners.

Most spiderlings are quick to move out on their own. Some of the web spinners form tiny hunting snares for the first time. Others begin hunting in the style of their species while still very small.

Spiderlings (and some adults) engage in a unique form of dispersal known as **ballooning**. Climbing up fence posts, branches or even blades of grass, they release silk from spinnerets. As the threads lengthen, the wind (even a slight breeze) catches the silk and lifts the little spider into

Ballooning begins with the spiderling raising its abdomen and shooting out silk threads. When a breeze catches the silk, they let go of their substrate and float away. Most flights are short; only a few feet.

the air as it floats, or "balloons" off to a new site (see illustration at bottom of page). Though ballooning can carry the small spiders long distances, the average flight may be only inches or a foot; usually to the next branch. Imagine flying a kite in a wind and letting a strong gust carry you away to a new home. Since many spiders, both young and old, disperse in the fall, ballooning is often associated with autumn. It can, however, take place any time from early spring to well after the leaf drop in late fall.

Indeed, with no leaves on the trees and the sun at a low angle, the clear days of late October are perfect for spotting the abandoned ballooning threads.

The spiderlings continue to grow through the next few weeks and in the style of all arthropods, they molt often. The old skin is shed, leaving behind an empty husk called **exuviae**. A typical spider molts from four to twelve times before it becomes an adult. The last stage before becoming an adult is called the **penultimate stage** (or just penultimate). Some spiders may not reach adulthood before late autumn and may winter as a penultimate, maturing in the spring. The stages of growth, those times between molts, are often called **instars**. For example the fourth instar would

The empty skin (called exuviae) of an immature spider is all that is left following a molt. True spiders do not molt as adults.

be the growth stage between the fourth and fifth molts. With each molt leading to adulthood, missing appendages, usually legs, can be regrown. However, once an adult, a spider is not capable of regenerating new appendages.

After completing the final molt from penultimate to adult, the spiders now have all the needed body parts to mate and reproduce. Also as an adult, they will not molt again. One of the differences between tarantulas (mygalomorphs) and the true spiders (araneomorphs) is that tarantulas molt as adults; true spiders do not.

Figure 1. Ballooning spider. Silk strands are released from the spinnerets in hopes that the wind will catch them and "balloon" the spiderling to new territory.

Courtship & Mating

Spiders exhibit strange behavior in a number of their life functions, but among the strangest are courtship and mating. Some of these unusual antics are due to the spider's anatomy. In the male, semen is produced in the testes that are located on the underside of the abdomen. When reaching adulthood and ready to mate, he builds a small "**sperm web**" where semen is placed. Here he inserts each palp bulb and fills up with semen. Remember, the palp (or pedipalp) is located near the male's face, looking almost like another short pair of legs. He is now ready to search for a receptive female. For mating to be complete, his palp needs to be inserted into her genital opening located near the epigynum on her undersides. To reach this area, the male usually needs to lay across her back (away from her jaws) and reach underneath her abdomen. To get this close, the normally much smaller male needs to court the female to let her know of his intent.

The smaller male *Araneus* orbweaver (left) approaches the larger female on her web with a series of vibrations and sequential movements that lets her know that he is not prey, but a suitor. He then must reach under her abdomen and inseminate her with the semen stored in his palp bulbs. The whole process is over in seconds.

Courtship varies depending on if the spider is a sedentary web-builder or an active-hunter. With the web-builders, eyesight is usually poor and it is easy for the bigger females to mistake the male for a meal. Because of this, he must approach on her web with a series of vibrations and movements in a sequence that lets her know that he is not prey, but a suitor. When close enough, he rapidly moves in for an instantaneous copulation and sperm transfer. With two palps full of semen, he performs this action twice in quick succession.

The tiny male Goldenrod Crab Spider cautiously approaches the much larger female. Courtship has begun.

Eyesight is considerably better among the wandering spiders, and so courtship is a more visual affair. Here the males may dance before the female, wave the palps or legs (or both) and take on strange poses. In our area, this can best be seen with the Salticidae (jumping spiders) and the Lycosidae (wolf spiders). Jumping spider males often have striking color patterns on their face and front legs. He performs a little dance for the female; raising and waving his front legs, palps or chelicerae while prancing back and forth. He carries on until the female notices and accepts him.

Fishing spiders (*Dolomedes*) also have a unique courtship. The male will vibrate his abdomen on the water's surface in a regular rhythm. The female will sense the even ripples on the water, knowing it is a male and not a struggling insect. Once they get together, a long period of leg-play takes place before they mate. Long-jawed orbweavers (*Tetragnatha*) approach each other in the web with jaws agape. The male has special spurs on his jaw which lock her jaws open. Now that she is immobilized he can inseminate her at will. But unfortunately, getting away after mating is not so easy, and some males are captured and eaten.

It is a popular misconception that the male is always killed and eaten by the female. This actually happens in only the *Tetragnatha* and very few other species. Mostly the sexes separate peaceably and the male may mate again. Indeed, sometimes they will share the same web or retreat for a while. Normally, however, the smaller male will die quickly after mating with the female.

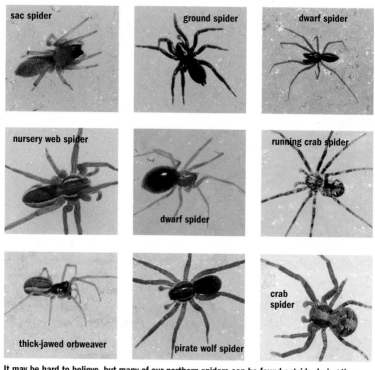

It may be hard to believe, but many of our northern spiders can be found outside during the winter. Here is just a sample of the many species I have photographed on the snow's surface.

Hunting

All spiders are predators and must hunt for their food. Most spiders can be divided into two groups: the web hunters and the active hunters.

When prey hits the web, the spider feels vibrations as the critter struggles to get free. Many moths, dragonflies and grasshoppers are strong enough to be able to escape the web. Typically, those not able to get away from the snare thrash about and get further entangled, struggling until they tire. The spider then moves in with an injection of venom that serves to subdue the prey and liquify its insides. If the spider is hungry, the food is devoured immediately; otherwise, the catch is wrapped in silk for a later meal.

Spiders that do not make webs get their prey in different ways. Some like the crab spiders (Thomisids) ambush prey by sitting still and using their camouflaged coloration. Others use good eyesight and quickness to pursue and capture prey. Such active hunters include the jumping spiders (Salticids), wolf spiders (Lycosids), nursery web spiders (Pisaurids), ground spiders (Gnaphosids) and running crab spiders (Philodromids). All use fangs and venom to subdue the prey and, just like the web-builders, they use enzymes to partially digest the victim's insides. Larger spiders proceed to crush the insect's exoskeleton as it is sucked dry.

Wintering

Winter is the time that we are least likely to find spiders, but they are present in one stage or another. We can even find them outside on the snow on mild winter days. As with any organism in this latitude, winter is a part of their life cycle, and spiders have different ways to deal with it.

Four winter-coping patterns seem to emerge for our northern spiders. A fifth pattern can be seen in those that take shelter indoors or in caves for all of their lives.

1. SPRING MATING. The spiders are adults in the spring and, after mating, form egg sacs in the summer. Immatures develop in the fall. After going through several molts, they winter as immatures in some stage of instar, often the penultimate. Example: Philodromidae (running crab spiders).

2. FALL MATING. These immature spiders of spring and summer reach adulthood in the fall. It is then that they mate and form egg sacs that survive the winter. Example: Araneidae (orbweavers).

3. WINTER MATING. The eggs of spring hatch to form young in summer and fall. They reach the adult stage in winter. Mating takes place at this time and egg sacs are produced. Example: Micryphantinae (dwarf spiders that live in the leaf litter under the snow).

4. SPRING OR FALL MATING. These spiders are actually quite similar to the first group except that some spiders may mature faster than others and become adults in the fall. They winter as adults and lay eggs in the spring. Others become adults in the spring.
Example: Lycosidae (wolf spiders).

5. MATE IN ANY SEASON. Spiders that live year round in man-made structures or natural caves live longer and can mate during any time of year. Example: Pholcidae (cellar spiders).

Though little research has been done in this area, it appears that the first pattern is most common in the North. Overwintering spiders are often immatures in one of the growth instars. Despite the cold of a North Woods winter, the snow cover and leaf litter seem to be adequate protection to allow spiders to survive. Activity slows, but they occasionally become more active on warm winter days. Immatures and adults of several species have been observed and collected on the snow's surface on mild days (see photos on previous page). Though observations have included many families of spiders, the most common ones seen in the winter include the Linyphiidae (sheetweb weavers), Micryphantinae (dwarf spiders), Lycosidae (wolf spiders), Philodromidae (running crab spiders) and Clubionidae (sac spiders). The occasional mild days between November and March may even bring out some ballooning spiders.

Leaf litter seems to be the most common wintering habitat of these spiders, but bark crevices, logs, out buildings and even our houses provide shelter for winter-active spiders.

Predators of Spiders

Spiders are predators. They catch and feed on other animals. In turn, however, they themselves are hunted and eaten as prey. The main predators of spiders are spiders. Many of the wandering hunting spiders will attack when they encounter another wandering spider. Sedentary web spinners will actively defend their own territories from other spiders.

Among the insects, wasps are perhaps the best-known and most effective spider predators. Two types of wasps, the spider wasps (family Pompilidae) and the mud daubers (family Sphecidae), specialize in these eight-footed critters. Both types of wasps attack the same way; they sting until the spider is paralyzed and then carry or drag it off to a hidden site (usually buried in the soil or placed in the nest). Once here, the wasp lays an egg on the spider's abdomen. After hatching, the wasp larva feeds on the living tissue of the paralyzed spider until the spider succumbs and the wasp pupates. In general, the spider wasps do not hunt particular species though some specialize on Araneids (orbweavers), Salticids (jumpers) or Lycosids (wolf spiders). Mud daubers mainly sting web spiders. The prey is enclosed in a natural cavity in soil or wood where it is sealed into mud tubes. The chambers look like little pipe organs. The paralyzed spiders serve as food only for the developing larvae and not the adults, which feed mostly on plant juices and nectar.

This Sphecid wasp paralyzes a spider with its sting. The wasp digs a hole in the sand where it buries the spider after laying an egg on its body. Developing wasp larva now have a handy food source.

Attacking spiders in a different way are the ichneuman wasps (family Ichneumidae) who will attach their eggs to live spiders or their egg sacs. Once here, the wasp larva lives as an ectoparasite. Various fly species will also seek out spiders for a similar parasitic relationship.

Vertebrate predators of spiders include fish, frogs, toads, salamanders, birds and small rodents. Many fish, particularly trout, eat spiders that happen to fall into rivers, ponds and lakes. Amphibians, though not abundant in the North Woods, do have a member, the American toad, that often feeds on spiders; in fact, spiders make up perhaps as much as five percent of its diet.

The influence of birds as a factor in controlling spider populations is generally overestimated. In winter, spiders tucked in bark crevices or under tree bark may be sought out and eaten by nuthatches, chickadees, kinglets, creepers and woodpeckers. Some are also fed to nestlings in the spring and summer. But for several reasons, spiders are lightly preyed-upon by birds. Here are some possible reasons:

Eat and be eaten. Spiders are preyed upon by several families of wasps. Here a crab spider becomes the victim.

• Most spider species are active at night when the majority of insect-eating birds are inactive.

• Spiders usually hide in retreats, whether they are web makers or not.

• Many are camouflaged and hard to see.

• Except for a few active hunters, most tend to sit still and are not likely to be perceived by birds.

• Spiders tend to be loners and finding a colony of spiders big enough to make a good meal does not happen very often.

Likewise, in the world of mammals, spiders do not make up a large portion of any animal's diet. In the North Woods it is most likely bats and the voracious shrew that consume spiders. Bats feed on spiders while on the wing and are even able to pick them up off the ground.

A bit of an indirect threat to spiders is theft; other critters that steal insects from spider webs. A few wasps and scorpion flies will trespass onto a web to take insect prey caught by the spiders. But possibly the best known thieves are the kleptoparasitic spiders of the genera *Argyrodes* and *Rhomphaea*. These members of the family Theriididae, (cobweb weavers) live on the orb webs of other species and steal their food.

Spider Observation

Spider watching is not yet as popular as bird watching or butterfly watching, but with a few tips on what to look for, when to look, where to look and their fascinating natural history, observation of these colorful arachnids can be quite rewarding.

For most of us, a spider sighting is merely a random occurrence–seeing a spider crawl over the sidewalk while we are mowing the lawn or catching a glimpse as one scampers away when we turn on the basement light.

More frequently, however, we see signs of the spiders in the form of webs in our windowsills, garages and gardens. Though spiders are nearly always solitary, by training our eyes and developing search patterns we will be able to observe many spiders and their behavior.

Spiders come in all shapes and sizes. A tiny Tuft-legged Orbweaver fits easily on a fingertip.

Optics for Observation

To view spiders more closely, either for our own sake or that of the spider, try one of these three optics:

CLOSE-FOCUS BINOCULARS. Binoculars that can focus on a critter from ten feet away or less are excellent for watching larger spiders in webs or on the water's surface.

CLOSE-UP CAMERA LENSES. Macro lenses or zoom lenses with extension tubes will both allow the observer to get a highly magnified image of spiders.

MAGNIFYING GLASSES. This may be the easiest method for viewing small spiders. Hold the magnifying glass near the spider, a foot or two from your eyes. These should not to be confused with hand lenses that are held close to one's eye. With a little practice, great viewing can be done with an ordinary five or ten magnification glass.

A quality magnifying glass will allow you a closer look into the world of spiders.

Web Watching

Perhaps the easiest place to view spiders is at their webs; and the ones we are most likely to see are circular orb webs. Orbweavers hatch in spring, and, after dispersal, each spiderling begins hunting on its own. Early summer webs are quite small, but as the spider grows, the snares get larger. By late summer, usually August, the female spider has reached maturity and her webs reach peak diameter.

Typically, the webs are constructed in the evening, shortly after dusk. As darkness falls, the spider emerges from its diurnal hiding-place to build a new web for another night of hunting. If the web happens to be near a house (often on a porch or deck), we may be able to watch the construction of their complex structure from the shelter of our home.

The cooler nights of late summer often result in morning dew or fog. Grasses and flowers, especially those in fields and meadows, become draped with condensation. The number of dew-covered webs seems beyond belief. All of last-night's webs are visible and quite spectacular. Put on your rubber boots and tramp a field or walk a trail to observe hundreds of webs as the sun rises in the background. Not only do orb webs abound,

Yellow Garden Argiopes hang upside down in their webs all day long. They make ideal subjects for observation and photography.

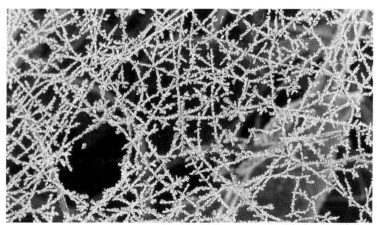

Don't stop spider watching when autumn arrives. Frosty mornings turn webs, such as this grass spider's funnel snare, into crystal lace.

but as we move into autumn, so do the funnel webs (abundant on mowed lawns) and sheet webs (easiest to see in shrubs). Marshes and swamp edges also hold a myriad of webs, including the orbs of the long-jawed orbweavers (*Tetragnatha*). Don't forget to check roadside fences, signs and mail boxes for webs, as well.

Nature photographers have made dew-covered spider webs a favorite subject for years and there is probably no aspect of the life of a spider that has received more aesthetic press. Diffuse lighting, calm conditions and a sparkling subject matter make these webs so photogenic. Stunning web photos have made their way onto many a magazine cover. Limited light in the morning, especially in fog, means slow shutter speeds and so a tri-pod is essential for any serious photographer of spider webs. Make sure to place the camera in the same plane as the web so it will be sharp across the whole photo. Also note that though orb webs appear to be flat, (nearly two dimensional), they

Dew-covered webs in the morning sunlight make for spectacular photographs, but their builders are rarely at home in such wet conditions.

actually have supporting threads coming in at other angles and so are not as easy to photograph as they appear. We need to grasp the moment because the dew, fog and the calm will not last.

Web viewing on late-summer mornings is easy, but seeing the web-maker is much harder. Usually the wet webs, though they make for good pictures, are not pleasant places for the spider to sit and they find dryer shelter in their retreat, behind a twig or in a nearby crack. Only a few spiders will stay in the middle of their web at this time. Anyone wanting to see or photograph the spider needs to study the web and nearby hiding sites to find the owner.

Spider watchers should be aware that most orbweavers, but not all, sit in the center of the web only after dark. Many of the *Argiope, Cyclosa* and *Mangora* spiders are exceptions and are likely to be seen during the day. In general, orb spiders are almost blind and so cannot see us; therefore, we can get quite close without being detected. Holding a magnifying glass at arm's length, close to the spider, can reveal great detail without disturbing the spider. Similar observation can be done at night with the addition of a flashlight. It is worth noting that though large *Araneus* spiders construct orb webs at dusk and hunt at night, many will run out of their retreats in the daytime to subdue prey such as grasshoppers, dragonflies and butterflies.

Adopting a web and regularly checking it as the spider constructs, destructs, repairs and then catches prey each day is a fascinating pastime. Besides being a valuable hunting device, the web is also the site of mating. Watch for that behavior as well. Orb weavers die in the cold weather so as we move towards first frost, they become less active.

Funnel webs (Agelenids), sheet webs (Linyphiids) and cobwebs (Theridiids and Pholcids) are often placed indoors and may remain intact for a long time. The spiders in these webs sit still and so can be readily observed, often for weeks on end. Spiders that have moved into our dwellings to construct their own homes help us control unwanted insects and are harmless.

Viewing Non-Web-Building Spiders

Magnifying glass viewing of spiders is a very effective technique for those wanting to see crab spiders and jumping spiders a bit closer. Crab spiders (Thomisids) make no web but can readily be seen in the open flowers of a summer meadow. Here they sit with outstretched legs as they blend in with the floral colors. Some crab spiders will change colors to become more cryptic. They remain white against the white background of a daisy or yarrow and then are able to turn yellow to match the petals of black-eyed susan and goldenrod. Though they possess better eyesight than the orb-weavers, they can often

Spiders can be observed in all facets of their life cycle. A fishing spider carries her egg sac as she goes about her daily business.

be approached closely with the use of a magnifying glass or a close-up lens of a camera. Any patch of daisies or black-eyed susans are worth a thorough search. Close-focus binoculars can be of great help here too.

Jumping spiders (Salticids) are active hunters like the wolf spiders (Lycosids). But unlike the Lycosids, they hunt during the daytime–often in direct sunlight. Walls, windows and tree trunks are favored sites, as are the leaves of plants like milkweed. With excellent eyesight, they patrol the area looking for nearby prey. As your magnifying glass nears the spider, it may look up with its two large, human-like front eyes and appear to be as interested in watching you as you are in watching them!

Nocturnal Adventures

Anyone serious about observing spiders needs to grab a flashlight or put on a headlamp and step outside into the night. Not only are web-building spiders active then, this is also the time when wolf spiders (Lycosids) travel on the ground. Likewise, night is when the large fishing spiders (*Dolomedes*) hunt along the water's edge. Both of these big, active-hunting spiders have eyes that reflect a flashlight's beam. When hit by the light, the two large eyes glow green from the ground. Such critters may be hard to get close to, and we may need to rely on close-focus binoculars

Though we seldom see the tiny spiderlings drifting in mid air, the threads that have been laid down in ballooning are commonly encountered.

for a better view. A nocturnal trip to a nearby dock on a lake will often turn up a few fishing spiders on the water, with the possibility of seeing a pirate wolf spider as well. Many long-jawed orbweavers (*Tetragnatha*) hang their webs on or near the dock. On a warm summer night, a single dock could harbor as many as one hundred *Tetragnatha* webs.

Photos taken at night are well worth the effort, but a camera with a close-up lens will also need an appropriate flash. As with any small animate subject, it is always best to take many pictures of each subject to insure success.

A very interesting part of the spider's life can be observed when the eggs hatch. The tiny spiders, known as spiderlings, feed on their stored yolk sac for a time and then disperse. This movement away from their siblings is critical because spiders are cannibals and will soon devour each other if they remain together for very long. Spiderlings climb up small twigs, posts, fences or even blades of grass and throw silk out into the air where a gust of a breeze or even rising thermals will carry off the thread and with it the adventurous spider. Such flights, known as "ballooning," may carry the young spider a fair distance, but usually flights are only a few inches to a couple feet. Though we seldom see the tiny spiderling drifting in mid air, the threads that have been laid down in ballooning are commonly encountered. The threads may be hard to see in the months when the leaves are on the trees but are readily apparent in the late autumn landscape of bare trees. Though spiders balloon all through the snow-free season, perhaps the easiest time for us to observe this behavior is during clear days of fall following the leaf drop. Brilliant blue-skied days of October, with the sun low, can reveal hundreds of threads in our yards or woods. Formerly the threads were called "goose hairs" or gossamer and clear warm days of October became known as "gossamer days".

Catching & Collecting

Field identification of many genera and species of spiders is extremely difficult and a specimen often needs to be examined under a stereomicroscope to be identified. Collecting spiders can be done in several ways:

SWEEP NETS. Probably the easiest way to collect large numbers of spiders with a limited diversity is to "sweep" a meadow on a sunny warm afternoon. Sweeping is done with the use of a special insect net. The devise consists of a canvas or cloth bag on a solid circular steel hoop that is attached to a long handle. The net is swept back and forth through the vegetation in a figure-eight pattern. Spiders live on the plants here and are knocked into the net, especially when the net is beat against the plants forcibly.

Once in the net, the caught critters (which are usually more insects than spiders) can be dumped into a clear box for sorting or just placed onto a white sheet or tarp where they are readily collected. Sweeping will no doubt reveal plenty of spiders, but it is most effective in fields, meadows or marsh habitats with mixed grasses and wild flowers. Many spiders are collected, but some groups are almost never seen in these sweep nets.

DROP CLOTH. Spiders that are arboreal can be obtained with the use of a drop cloth spread on the ground beneath a tree or bush. Knocking the limbs of the tree with a stick or shaking the branches will dislodge insects and spiders to fall onto the cloth. A light-colored canvas works best. Specimens are easily taken from the cloth.

TULLGREN FUNNEL. The abundant spiders of the forest floor leaf litter are likely to be missed in collecting by sweep nets or ground cloths. These tiny spiders can be collected with the use of a funnel device known as a Tullgren funnel. (A similar collector is called the Berlease funnel.)

Here's how it works: Forest floor leaves, needles and duff are collected and brought indoors in a plastic bag or bucket. Here the material is put in the top of a funnel with a wire screen beneath. A heat source such as a 45-watt bulb is placed above the leaf litter. As the light bulb dries and warms the sample, small arthropods including spiders, move deeper into the layer of leaves until they fall through the bottom screen, down the funnel and into a jar or tray. Those wanting to save this collection will place a jar of isopropyl alcohol beneath to preserve the spiders.

PITFALL TRAPS. A variety of wandering spiders and other arthropods can be collected with the use of a pitfall trap. These devices are especially effective for capturing nocturnal spiders. Though the design varies greatly, pitfall traps basically consist of a can sunk into the ground so that the upper edge is flush with the ground's surface. Within the can, a cup is placed in the bottom and a funnel on top. Critters moving around on the ground will fall into the funnel and the cup below. A smooth surface prevents their escape. Many collectors have had success using a plastic one-liter pop bottle. The top one-third or so is cut off and reversed into the lower part to become a funnel. Collecting cups can be placed inside and below the funnel. Once again, a preservative, usually isopropyl alcohol, is placed in the cup for those desiring a permanent catch. Pitfall traps should have a raised board placed above the sunken can or bottle. This allows for movement of the spiders active on the ground, but keeps out rain.

INDIVIDUAL COLLECTING JARS. A slower but more meticulous way of collecting spiders is to place them one by one in small jars or vials. Alcohol in these collecting jars can preserve any finds. Such vials should be labeled as to where and when collected.

Live spiders should be kept separate from each other. Spiders are antisocial and cannibalistic (the ultimate antisocial behavior!), and they will readily attack and eat each other. Placing a cloth or paper towel inside the jar will give them a place to hide from each other and so several live spiders can be carried, at least for a while, within the same container.

Insect collections are common and most of us have seen these pinned specimens in boxes. Pinning works fine for insects, but not for spiders. Anyone wishing to make a permanent reference collection of spiders should not pin their specimens. The soft abdomens do not dry well and will shrivel and be worthless as a reference.

Many spider preservatives are used in museum collections. Probably the best known is to place each spider, or species of spider, in its own vial of non-denatured ethyl alcohol. Since this may be difficult to obtain, you can use isopropyl alcohol instead (it is readily available at stores). Labels should always be printed with pencil, not pen.

Living spiders can be maintained quite easily for considerable periods of time as long as they are kept in separate containers. Any glass or plastic jars, if large enough, may be used as a spider cage. Ventilation can be provided by a cloth or screened top. For more extensive periods of captivity, you may want to construct a terrarium with rocks, plants and water. Spiders can live many days without being fed but soon die without water. A small piece of moistened sponge is adequate if kept wet. Most spiders readily accept fruit flies, crickets or other small insects as food.

Orbweavers when collected in the fall may make egg sacs, but even if fed, they are not likely to live long. Many specimens of wolf spiders, fishing spiders, jumping spiders and some web spiders have been kept alive for considerable time in captivity if taken care of properly.

After examining, identifying or photographing your captive spiders, release them back to the habitat where they were caught.

Spiders are amazing critters that can be observed throughout much of the year. As we learn more about them and their amazing life history, their little eight-legged personalities come alive. When we know more about them, our spider neighbors become less scary. They are creatures that are not only harmless to us but are actually of great benefit. Please think twice about smashing a spider in the house. Gently capture it and let it go outside if you don't want it indoors. I hope this book increases your wonder and curiosity about the spiders of the North Woods. Take it into the woods with you. Pack it in your daypack for your next hike. Keep a copy handy in the house to identify your house spiders. Spider watching can be a fascinating hobby. I hope you will join me in the journey.

The intricate handiwork of spiders is all around us. Get to know them better through careful observation.

How to use this Field Guide

Spiders of the North Woods is designed to make field identification easier for you, the reader. Through the use of color photos, arrows pointing to field marks, size scales and habitats, we have made a handy, compact and easy to use guide. It is small enough to tuck in any daypack.

We have made no attempt to include all species, or even all the genera, of the North Woods' spider fauna. Instead, we have highlighted some of the most common, several of the bizarre, a few of the most colorful and, yes, even a couple poisonous spiders that are at the fringe of their range.

For the purposes of this book we will define the North Woods as the area underlain by the granite of the Canadian Shield. This would encompass northeast Minnesota, northern Wisconsin, the Upper Peninsula of Michigan, parts of Ontario, Quebec and New England.

This book focuses on Minnesota, Wisconsin and Michigan. But remember, not all species are found in any single area. Habitat preferences tend to spread these species out. The North Woods is a mosaic of preferred spider habitats; from lakes, marshes and rivers to deciduous woods, boreal forests, meadows, suburban yards, flower gardens and homesteads. And don't forget the inside of your own home; spiders are year-round residents of even the tidiest houses.

Organization

Spiders–order Araneae–are organized by families and then broken down further into genera, and where possible, species. We have arranged the spider families in standard scientific order except that the six-eyed spider families have been moved to the back. Within each family, the genera are simply arranged alphabetically.

With experience in the field using this guide, you will gradually learn to identify spiders to family.

Spider Names

Like all organisms, spiders are given a scientific name. Unfortunately, many spiders do not have a common name. The common names are the English names most amateur naturalists use, while the scientific or Latin names tend to be the spoken word of entomologists and arachnologists. In this book we list all spiders according to the *Common Names of Arachnids 1995,* a booklet put out by the American Arachnological Society. One exception is the family Pholcidae which the *Common Names of Arachnids 1995* lists as "daddy longlegs spiders". We feel this is confusing for the lay person who immediately thinks of the long-legged harvestman, or daddy longlegs, that are so common around our homes. Harvestmen are arachnids but are not spiders. They belong to the order Opiliones. We refer to members of the Pholcidae as cellar spiders.

When no common name exists for a species of spider, we have manufactured one from the Latin specific epitath. For example, *Steatoda borealis*, a species of cobweb weaver which has no common name, becomes the Northern Cobweb Weaver as "borealis" refers to the North. When the Latin specific epitath has no relevant meaning we simply call the spider by the group name with a "sp." afterwards (short for "species"). For example, *Dolomedes scriptus* becomes "Fishing Spider sp." or, in other words, a species of fishing spider.

All common names referring to a specific species will be capitalized. For example, "black widow" is not capitalized because it can refer to several species such as "Northern Widow" and "Southern Black Widow."

The family name is listed at the bottom of all the species account pages. In the case of the family Linyphiidae, the subfamily is listed on the right hand page.

Arrows highlight easily recognizable features to aid in identification.

Black size-bars show estimated legspan of males (M) and females (F). From the white bar to the left edge of size-bar is body length.

Photos on the right side of the spread highlight webs, hunting techniques, sexual dimorphism and/or unique behaviors.

Spiders of the North Woods

Goldenrod Crab Spider *Misumena vatia* (female)

Meadows, fields and gardens. Often on goldenrods and daisies.

Nature Notes:
I have found that nearly every patch of daisies has one or two resident Goldenrod Crab Spiders during June.

Females and males look very different and it is easy to think that they represent different species. He is tiny! (See photo on page 21.)

Courting and mating take place on the same flowers that the females hunt from.

Females on flowers are often photographed.

Spiders grab prey with the front legs, but continue to hold and feed on the insect without use of the legs.

Description: Female's body is 8 to 10 mm long. Male's is 3 to 4 mm. Legspans range from 8 to 20 mm.

Abdomen: White or yellow with pink-red wavy bands ↑ running down each side. Can change color from white to yellow to light green. Such a change takes several days. Male's abdomen is pale with dark edges and two median lines.

Carapace: Female's carapace is colored the same as the abdomen usually white. Eye region may be tinged with red. Male's carapace is dark reddish-brown to red with a light spot in middle extending from the eyes.

Legs: Same color as the body. Pairs one and two are the longest and held out crab-like ↑. These legs are extremely long in the male.

Hunting Technique: Hunts during daylight hours by ambushing prey. Able to camouflage itself by changing from white to pale green to match the flower it is hunting on.

Goldenrod Crab Spider and honey bee in a life and death struggle on an Ox-eye Daisy. The spider has remained white to blend in with the white petals.

Prefers to hunt from yellow and white flowers; ox-eye daisy and black-eyed susans in early summer, goldenrods later.

Web: None.

Egg Sac & Eggs: Eggs sacs are attached to leaves.

Life cycle: Mature in early summer after which, mating takes place. Adults can be seen most of the summer. Overwinter as immatures.

A crab spider waits at the entrance of a Showy Ladyslipper orchid.

A female Goldenrod Crab Spider attaches her egg sac to a folded leaf.

Nature Notes **are natural history tidbits about that species.**

Habitats where the spider is generally found are listed here.

Family name in Latin and English is listed on the bottom of each page.

Family Characteristics

At the beginning of each family is a two-page spread that describes their unifying characteristics. Study these traits as they are generally not repeated in each genus/species text. Illustrated next to the text is a silhouette of a typical member of the family, a generic face showing chelicerae style and eye placement and a dorsal view of the carapace or view of the spinnerets. A shaded silhouette shows the actual size of a typical female. If it is a web-building family, then a generic web is shown. Other diagnostic family traits may be illustrated as well.

Photos & Illustrations

Most photos are by the author and taken in northern Minnesota and Wisconsin. (Photo credits are listed in Appendix D.) Since female spiders are almost always larger and more obvious, it is usually the females we have chosen to illustrate. Males are shown in genera/species accounts where they are commonly seen, as in the Salticidae (jumping spiders).

Illustrations show facets of spider anatomy and natural history that are very difficult to photograph. All illustrations are by Rick Kollath.

Fieldmark Arrows

Arrows point to diagnostic features in the photos which are referenced in the description text and marked with an arrow symbol (↑). These are characteristics that you should look for while in the field. Jotting down notes on bands, spots, colors and other abdomen, carapace and leg patterns will help you identify the spider when you have a chance to consult this book.

Habitat

Preferred habitat is found beneath the spider's main photo. These are the places where that particular genus/species can most likely be found.

Nature Notes

Nature Notes are Larry's personal observations on spider natural history that bring one a more complete understanding of that species. Unique behavior, phenology, range and prey choice are just some of the topics touched on.

Species Text

Description begins with a size range of the female's and male's body in millimeters. With spiders we are often describing very small species and inches just don't cut it. Legspan is next. Most of us describe a spider by its entire span, not just its body size. Since there is very little literature on the extended length of spiders, Larry has estimated the natural resting legspan of the typical full adult male and female. The black size-bars on the main photo represent this legspan.

Within each size-bar is a white bar. From the white bar to the left edge of the size-bar is the actual body length of a full adult of that species. This is only attempted for the larger spiders.

As far as body parts, the abdomen is described first because that is what most people notice first. Females are described and, if males are commonly seen, they are also discussed. Carapace traits are next. Eye placement and size is covered in the family text at the start of the chapter. They are only described under genus/species accounts if it is a visible defining characteristic. Leg description usually centers on length, whether annulated (ringed) or not and if they are spined or hairy.

Under **Hunting Technique**, Larry discusses methods the spider employs to get its prey. Web design is not discussed here but under the next header.

Webs is where we learn what style of hunting snare is made by the spider. Active hunting spiders do not make webs at all, but may make silken retreats or nurseries. These are mentioned here as well.

Egg Sac & Eggs may touch on several topics; when eggs are laid, what the egg sac looks like, where they are placed and whether they are guarded by the female or not.

Life Cycle speaks to when that spider reaches adulthood, when courtship occurs, when eggs are laid and how they spend the winter.

Glossary

Spider biology is an area of science loaded with technical jargon. Identification often requires the use of many of these words. Check out page 194 for the easy-to-understand meanings of some tricky terms.

Titles of Interest & Additional References

This list of recommended reading and resources includes our favorite titles for delving deeper into the fascinating world of the arachnids. Also listed are books on close-up nature photography. Appendix A.

Appendix B. lists more technical references that the author consulted in his research.

Spider Conservation Groups & Websites

Few people are serious students or hobbyists of spiders. If you want to pursue your study of the eight-legged ones, here are some arachnid connections you can make.

Enjoy *Spiders of the North Woods*. Take it in the field. Cram it in your pack. Use it. But most importantly, have fun getting to know our fascinating northern spiders.

Cellar Spiders
Family Pholcidae

Cellar spiders are probably best known as the spiders with long legs and small bodies that hang in cobwebs in dark corners of buildings, especially basements, cellars and attics.

Description

Medium-sized spiders (6 to 10mm) with light-colored bodies and very long legs.

Abdomen: Elongated and light-colored; whitish, gray or pale yellow.

Carapace: Circular and light-colored; whitish, gray or pale yellow.

Eyes: Small anterior median eyes (AME); the other six are larger and grouped in two triads.

Legs: Very long and thin; five times the body length!

Similar Spiders

Theridiids (cobweb weavers) also hang inverted in cobwebs, but their legs are much shorter, and the spiders have more color patterns. Due to the cellar spider's long, thin legs, they could be also be confused with the daddy longlegs, or harvestman, which are not spiders (order Opiliones) and have only one body part, no venom and build no web.

Habitat

Often found indoors. Commonly live in basements; hence the common name of cellar spider.

Web

An irregular web, often called "cobweb", is constructed in dark corners of houses and other buildings and serves as a hunting snare. Threads appear tangled with no apparent order.

Hunting Technique

Cellar spiders hang inverted in their cobweb and can be seen almost any time of day or night. Males and females may be found together.

Observations

When alarmed, they shake rapidly and appear as a blur in the web. May survive the winter indoors.

Egg Sac & Eggs

Egg sac is wrapped with only a few threads. It is held by the female in her chelicerae as she is in the web.

Diversity

About 35 species are found in North America. One genus in this guide.

Pholcus

Cellar Spiders (Family Pholcidae)

40 Long-bodied Cellar Spider (*Pholcus*)

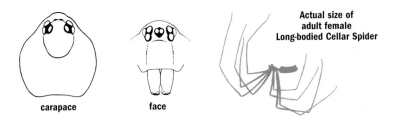

**Actual size of
adult female
Long-bodied Cellar Spider**

carapace

face

Irregular web or "cobweb" of family Pholcidae spiders

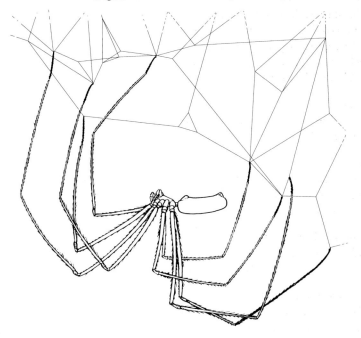

Long-bodied Cellar Spider *Pholcus phalangiodes*

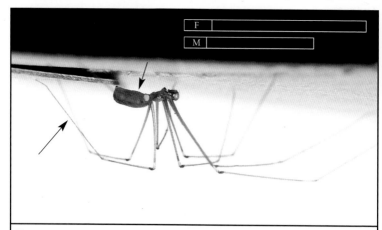

Hang upside down in an irregular web, or cobweb, in cellars, basements, attics, dark corners and caves.

Nature Notes:

I have often found these spiders in webs in corners of buildings throughout the winter.

Sometimes these spiders are called by the confusing name of "daddy longleg spiders". What most people think of as a "daddy longlegs" is actually a species of harvestman and not a spider at all! (See page 1).

Description: Female's body is 7 to 8 mm long. Male's is 5 to 6 mm long. Legspans range from 35 to 50 mm.

Abdomen: Elongated and almost tubular ↑; more than twice as long as wide. More than twice the length of the carapace. Pale gray with darker dorsal markings.

Carapace: Almost circular. Pale yellow with gray markings in center.

Eyes: Males have eyes raised above the rest of the carapace.

Legs: Extremely long and thin ↑. The legs may superficially resemble those of daddy longlegs (harvestmen of order Opiliones). Femur of the first pair may be five times the length of the carapace.

Hunting Technique: These spiders hang inverted in their cobweb and can be seen almost any time of day or night. Males and females can be found together.

Web: Irregular cobwebs. Spider hangs upside-down in the web. When disturbed, it may shake its body to appear as a blur.

Egg Sac & Eggs: The egg sac is coated with just a few threads and is held by the female in the web.

Life Cycle: They can be found indoors throughout most of the year; especially the females.

Cobweb Weavers (Comb-footed Spiders)
Family Theridiidae

Members of the family Theridiidae are best known as the spiders with rounded abdomens that hang inverted in cobwebs; often indoors.

Description

Medium-sized spiders (3 to 15 mm) of various colors. The abdomen is usually rounded. Spiders hang upside-down in irregular webs.

Abdomen: Glossy. Usually globular, oval or pointed. Various color patterns.

Carapace: Flat, short and usually glossy with few hairs.

Eyes: Anterior median eyes (AME) are small and dark; others are pearly.

Legs: Medium to long and slender; uniformly colored or banded. Legs have some spines and hairs; six to ten slightly curved bristles on hind tarsi and three claws. These tiny tarsi hairs explain why the Theridiids are sometimes called comb-footed spiders.

Chelicerae: Jaws have no teeth.

Similar Spiders

Linyphiids (sheetweb weavers) also hang inverted in their webs, but theirs is not a cobweb as with the Theridiids. Linyphiids are also thinner with longer legs and robust chelicerae with teeth.

Habitat

Low plants, dry fields, tree trunks, burrows and stone walls. Easiest to see in or near buildings.

Hunting Technique

Cobweb weavers are sedentary hunters, hanging upside down in the center of irregular webs or hiding nearby. Using tiny combs made of bristles at the end of the fourth leg, the spiders throw viscid silk over captured insects. Prey may be dragged to the sitting site of the web. Spiders do most of their hunting at night.

Web

Hunting snares are cobwebs of irregular strands. Outer threads are sticky. A sheet may be in the middle, and a tunnel-like passageway may be present too. Webs are placed in protected sites. Sometimes abundant in or near buildings where every corner or windowsill may have these irregular webs.

Observations
May remain active late in the season; some even overwinter indoors. Males pluck threads of females to initiate courtship. Females living in their web with dozens of hatched young is the closest thing to social spider behavior as we have in the North Woods.

Egg Sac & Eggs
Egg sacs are round, brown and paper-like. Sacs are suspended in the web near the resting site and guarded by the females.

Diversity
About 230 species are found in North America. Four genera in this guide.

Achaearanea
Rhomphaea
Steatoda
Theridion

Cobweb Weavers (Family Theridiidae)
44 Common House Spider (*Achaearanea*)
46 Lizard Spider *(Rhomphaea)*
47 Social Cobweb Weaver species (*Theridion)*
48 Northern Cobweb Weaver (*Steatoda*)

Cobweb typical of the Theridiidae

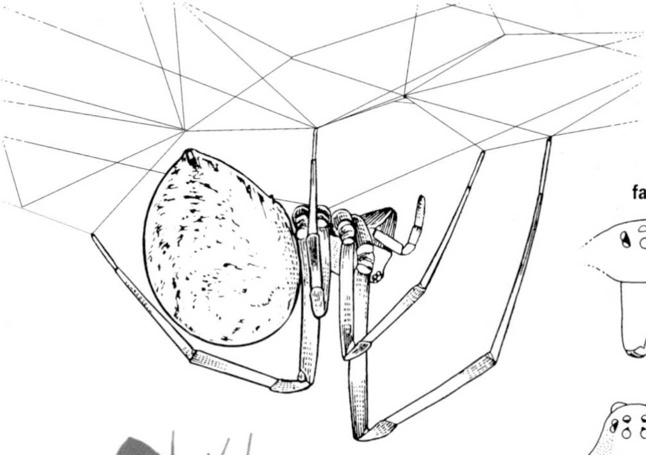

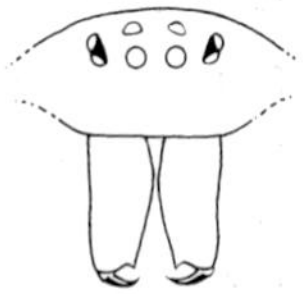

**Actual size of adult female
Common House Spider**

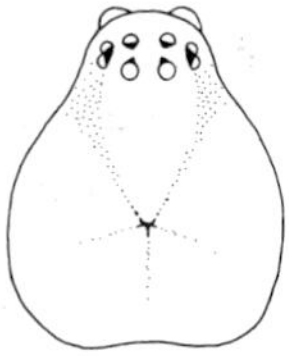

face

carapace

Common House Spider *Achaearanea tepidariorum*

Sheltered corners of houses, barns, garages and other buildings. Corners of rooms and angles of windows. Also under stones, boards, bridges and on fences.

Nature Notes:

A cosmopolitan spider that is found across the northern hemisphere.

Male and female may be in the same web at the same time.

Often seen in or near houses. Several can usually be seen on the outside of buildings during late-summer nights. They hide in their retreat during the day.

Description: Female's body is 6 to 8 mm long. Male's is 4 to 5 mm. Legspans range from 15 to 20 mm.

Abdomen: Large and bulbous with a down-pointing terminal end ↑. Dirty white to brown with indistinct gray chevrons on posterior half. Patches and streaks of black on the sides. Mottled-looking. Male's abdomen is tiny in comparison.

Carapace: Yellowish-brown; middle is darker brown.

Legs: Female's are yellow with dusky rings. Male's are orangish.

Hunting Technique: Most hunting is done at night. Sits upside down in the cob web. Spider wraps ensnared prey in silk. Retreat into cracks or corners during the day.

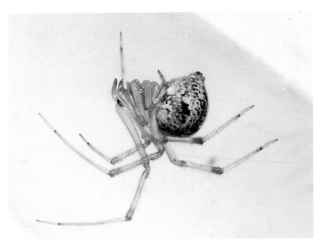

The **Common House Spider**, with its bulbous abdomen and long legs, superficially resembles an orbweaver but they weave cobwebs instead of orbs.

Web: Irregular cobweb with sticky strands. Spider sits inverted in the web. Abandoned webs are commonly seen in buildings. Male and female may be in the same web at the same time.

Egg Sac & Eggs: Pear-shaped brownish egg sac hangs in web during the summer.

Life Cycle: Adult females can live for more than a year. Adults can be found at any time of the year.

An adult cricket makes a good meal for a female Common House Spider. Most spiders can survive for two weeks on a single meal.

Lizard Spider *Rhomphaea lacerta* (a.k.a *Argyrodes fictilium*)

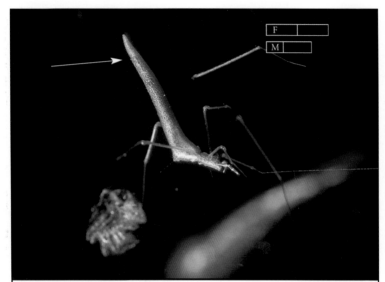

Often these spiders live in the periphery of other spider's webs, such as the orb webs of Araneidae. In bushes and trees.

Nature Notes:

The Latin name *lacerta* means "lizard"; referring to its abdomen shape.

Also known as *Argyrodes fictilium* .

Mostly a southern spider but it is found in the North Woods. This one was photographed on my land in northern Minnesota.

Description: Female's body is 5 to 9 mm long. Male's is 4 to 7 mm. Legspans range from 12 to 16 mm.

Abdomen: Long and thin; almost worm-like ↑; extending well beyond the spinnerets. Uniformly light yellow with a silvery sheen.

Carapace: Short. Light yellowish.

Legs: Long and thin. Uniformly light yellow.

Hunting Technique: Kleptoparasites. Lizard Spiders live in the webs of other spiders and feed on their host's caught prey. Occasionally make their own web.

Web: Though some make small irregular webs of their own, most live in the webs of other spiders.

Egg Sac & Eggs: Vase-like egg sacs are hung in their own webs.

Life Cycle: Adults appear in summer. Probably overwinter as immatures.

Social Cobweb Weaver sp. *Theridion* species

Low plants, tall grasses and bushes at the edge of woods.

Description: Female's body is 2 to 4 mm long. Male's is 1 to 3 mm. Legspans range from 5 to 8 mm.

Abdomen: Large and ovoid. Many *Theridion* species have a light arrowhead-shaped medial strip on a darker abdomen ↑.

Carapace: Small. Light-colored to orangish with a narrow to wide dark band in center.

Legs: Long and thin with spines and hairs. Pale yellow or white.

Chelicerae: Jaws are yellow.

Hunting Technique: Spider hangs inverted in the web waiting for small snared insects.

Web: Small irregular web. Usually found on the undersides of leaves, in shrubs and tall grasses. Webs are a few inches to three feet or more above the ground.

Egg Sac & Eggs: Spherical sacs are fastened to the web or placed underneath leaves where they are guarded by the female.

Life Cycle: Spiders mature in spring. Adults are found throughout the summer. Egg sacs in summer. Winter is spent as an immature.

Nature Notes:

We often think of Theridiidae webs as only being found indoors, but those of genus *Theridion* may be built far from buildings.

Mother may tolerate the spiderlings living in her web for a short while after they hatch.

Northern Cobweb Weaver   *Steatoda borealis*

F |
M |

Can be common under eaves of cabins, barns, sheds, bridges, corners of buildings and basements. Also under bark, stones and in rock crevices.

Nature Notes:

Very common around eaves of homes, cabins, outhouses and window sills (inside and out).

I have often seen adults in webs late in the season. Even in the winter, spiders will make webs indoors.

Description: Female's body is 6 to 8 mm long. Male's is 5 to 6 mm. Legspan ranges from 12 to 15 mm.

Abdomen: Glossy and oval. Dark with light dashed band running down the middle ↑. This band joins with a light transverse band forming a T-shape near the anterior end.

Carapace: Glossy orange-brown with short hairs.

Eyes: AME (anterior median eyes) are the largest.

Legs: Almost as dark as the carapace.

Hunting Technique: Spider sits in a crevice near the web, or sometimes in the web, waiting for insect prey.

Northern Cobweb Weavers will stay active all through the winter indoors. Note the glossy sheen on their body and pale lines running down the middle of the abdomen.

Web: An irregular sheet, as is characteristic with all members of this family. But this spider also adds threads above and below the sheet to knock insects into the main web.

Egg Sac & Eggs: Egg sacs are formed in summer.

Life Cycle: Adults and all stages of young can be found during all seasons of the year. Mating takes place in the spring. Female and male may live together on the same web. Egg sacs formed in summer. They may winter indoors.

Sheetweb Weavers
Family Linyphiidae (Subfamily Linyphiinae)

Sheetweb weavers are best known by their domed or bowl-shaped webs that are seen in shrubs. Most abundant and visible during the foggy days of late summer. Usually they have thin bodies and hang inverted under the sheet webs.

Description
Mostly small spiders (less than 7 mm). Sheetweb weavers are classified as a subfamily (Linyphiinae) by many authorities.

Abdomen: Longer than wide. Often with a light-dark pattern.

Carapace: Flat and ovoid. Can be dark or light in color with few, if any, patterns.

Eyes: Nearly all equal in size. Two parallel rows of four eyes each.

Legs: Long and thin. Spiny with strong setae and three claws.

Chelicerae: Strong with teeth.

Similar Spiders
Theridiids (cobweb weavers) have a shorter, rounded abdomen, no leg spines and no chelicerae teeth. Micryphantids (dwarf weavers) are smaller with shorter abdomens, but are also members of the family Linyphiidae.

Habitat
Abundant in woodlands and grasslands. Prefer shady sites; bushes, small conifers and edges of swamps.

Web
Hunting snare is a dome-shaped, bowl-shaped or flat web with no retreat. Spiders hang inverted beneath the platform; some make a second platform below them. The web is usually placed between branches of bushes or grasses. The web seems huge compared to the spider. No molting webs or egg-sac webs are built.

Hunting Technique
As a sedentary hunter, the sheetweb weavers hang upside down at the base of their webs. Here they bite and pull insect prey down through the platform. Webs are most abundant in late summer.

Observations
Spiders run rapidly when disturbed. Spiders remain active late in the season and are often seen ballooning in autumn. Occasionally seen on the snow's surface.

Egg Sac & Eggs

Egg sacs are placed near, or attached to, their webs.

Diversity

About 250 species are found in North America. Three genera in this guide.

Frontinella
Neriene
Pityohyphantes

Sheetweb Weavers (Family Linyphiidae/Subfamily Linyphiinae)

52 Bowl-and-Doily Weaver (*Frontinella*)
54 Filmy Dome Spider (*Neriene*)
56 Hammock Spider (*Pityohyphantes*)

face   **carapace**

**Actual size of adult female
Filmy Dome Spider**

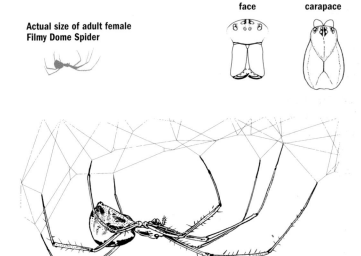

**Sheetweb weavers usually hang inverted
below sheet-like webs**

Bowl-and-Doily Weaver *Frontinella pyramitela*

F ▭
M ▭

Pine woods, bushes, tall grasses and yard shrubs. Often at the edges of woodlands.

Nature Notes:

Female and male may share the same web.

Dew-covered webs are often visible on summer mornings creating great photo opportunities.

One of several Linyphiids that are seen late in the season.

Frequently found on the snow.

Description: Female's body is 3 to 4 mm long. Male's is 2 to 3 mm. Legspans range from 9 to 12 mm.

Abdomen: Oblong and about as high above the spinnerets as it is in front. Black with light pattern that is often connected to vertical lines on the sides. Yellow spots are seen along the lower sides of the abdomen ↑. When seen from above, a dark band separates the lighter patterns.

Carapace: Small when compared to the abdomen. Evenly dark brown.

Legs: Long and slender. Pale yellowish-tan.

Chelicerae: Five or six teeth on jaws.

Hunting Technique: Insects hit the tangle of guy lines and fall into the bowl-shaped web. The spider, who is waiting patiently, clinging upside-down under the bowl, reaches up and pulls the victim through the bottom. It then

The "bowl-and-doily" web is a beautiful creation. Insects hit the tangle of guy lines and fall into the bowl-shaped web. The spider, who is waiting patiently, clinging upside down under the bowl, reaches up and pulls the victim through the bottom. It then brings it to the flat web or "doily" to eat in peace.

brings it to the flat web or "doily" to eat in peace.

Web: A fascinating two-parted sheet web. One part of the web is in the shape of a bowl and placed above another horizontal sheet web platform (the doily). Above the web is a maze of threads that deflect insects into the bowl. Our spider rests below the bowl and waits. Web is often two to three feet above the ground.

Egg Sac & Eggs: Produced in summer.

This is the upside-down position that Bowl-and-Doily Spiders assume as they patiently wait for victims.

Life Cycle: Adults can be found throughout the summer. Maturity is reached in the spring. Ballooning is common among the young.

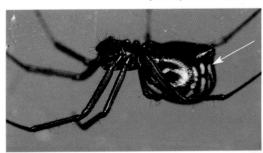

Filmy Dome Spider *Neriene radiata*

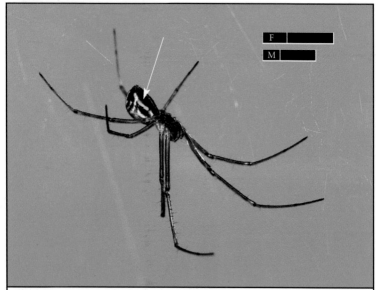

F
M

Woodlands, especially in the underbrush. Rock piles and stone walls as well.

Nature Notes:

Formerly known as *Prolinyphia marginata*.

Dew-covered dome webs are highly photogenic.

Like other Linyphiids, they sometimes remain active well into the fall.

Description: Female's body is 4 to 6.5 mm long. Male's is 3.5 to 5 mm. Legspans range from 15 to 20 mm.

Abdomen: Widest and highest behind the midpoint. Dark median stripe with wavy edges. Often shows a pair of white spots on the posterior end of the abdomen. Yellow dashes along lower edges of abdomen connect to white side stripes ↑. Venter is dark.

Carapace: Dark brown with broad white lateral margins.

Legs: Very long. All legs are light yellow.

Chelicerae: Three cheliceral teeth.

Hunting Technique: Spider hangs inverted underneath the top of the dome web. No retreat is made. The tangle of threads above the dome are intended to knock small insects to the main web. Insects are pulled through the dome and eaten.

This picture is not upside down! The Filmy Dome Spider makes an inverted bowl-shaped web amongst shrubs and taller plants. The webs are nearly invisible until water droplets condense on the threads in foggy conditions.

Web: Dome-shaped sheet web surrounded by a maze of threads. Dome is about four to six inches in diameter. Webs are within a few feet of the ground.

Egg Sac & Eggs: Egg sac is attached to leaves or other objects near the web.

Life Cycle: Maturity is reached in spring. Mating and egg-laying occurs throughout the summer. Male and female may live together in the same web. Overwinters as an immature spider.

The spider hangs inverted under the dome waiting for insect prey. Victims are pulled through the dome.

Hammock Spider   *Pityohyphantes costatus*

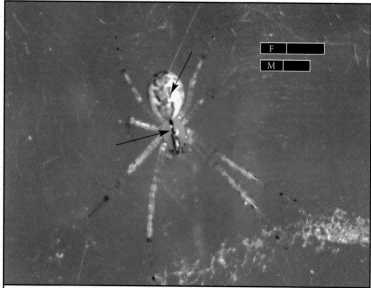

Webs often under the eaves of buildings, outhouses, on fences, low tree limbs and bushes. Woods, shrubby areas and fields.

Nature Notes:

This is another Linyphiid that may be active late into the fall; either in or away from webs.

Description: Female's body is 5 to 7 mm long. Male's is 4.5 to 6 mm. Legspans range from 14 to 18 mm.

Abdomen: Light with median dark herringbone pattern ↑ enclosing some light spots. Sides are pale or white.

Carapace: Light with median dark, forked-stripe extending from middle eyes down the length of the carapace ↑.

Legs: Yellow with rings and spots.

Hunting Technique: Spider lies in wait below a corner of the web or in the nearby retreat.

Web: Flat sheet of random intricate mesh with a maze of barrier strands above. Webs are placed on cabins, fences, outbuildings, shrubs or lower tree limbs. Often a leaf that has fallen into the web is curled to form a retreat.

Egg Sac & Eggs: Sacs are placed on the web.

In typical sheetweb weaver fashion, the Hammock Spider hangs inverted below its web.

Life Cycle: Mature in spring. Adults mate in early summer. Egg sacs are produced in early summer. Adults and nearly-grown young hibernate under rocks or bark.

Note the pale sides and dark herringbone pattern on the abdomen that are characteristic of this species.

Dwarf Spiders
Family Linyphiidae (Subfamily Micryphantinae)

Dwarf spiders were formerly in their own family called Micryphantidae (or Erigonidae). They have now been lumped with the sheetweb weavers in the family Linyphiidae. The subfamily is sometimes called Erigoninae. This subfamily of tiny spiders is probably best known for their habit of ballooning in the fall.

Description

Tiny spiders (less than 3 mm).

Abdomen: Spherical. Abdomen may have shiny plates.

Carapace: May be as wide as long and red or black. Some males have eyes on turrets.

Eyes: Two above; a lower row of six in three pairs.

Legs: Short with setae and spines. Three claws.

Similar Spiders

Sheetweb weavers have many similar characteristics but are larger and make bigger webs in bushes and shrubs; not found as much in the leaf litter.

Habitat

Abundant amongst dead leaves on the ground and under stones. More common away from the tropics. May be the most abundant family of spiders in the North Woods; thousands per acre.

Web

Hunting snares are small sheet webs; made on or near the ground.

Hunting Technique

Dwarf spiders capture tiny fauna in tiny sheet webs.

Observations

Because of their small size and habitat, they are not usually seen by people. Frequent ballooner in autumn. Sometimes seen on the surface of the snow.

Egg Sac & Eggs

Egg sac is a flat, white or yellow-white circle in the leaf litter.

Diversity

About 600 species are found in North America. Two genera in this guide.

> *Erigone*
> *Hypselistes*

Dwarf Spiders (Family Linyphiidae/Subfamily Micryphantinae)

> 60 Black Dwarf Spider species (*Erigone*)
> 61 Splendid Dwarf Spider (*Hypselistes)*

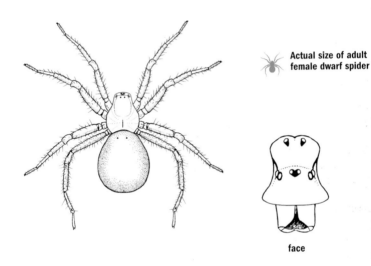

Actual size of adult female dwarf spider

face

Black Dwarf Spider sp. *Erigone* species

Under dead leaves, rocks and debris on the ground. May be abundant in such sites. Rarely seen by the casual observer.

Nature Notes:

Note the elm seed in the photo above. It gives us an idea of how tiny these spiders actually are.

Because of their diminutive size, the dwarf spiders use ballooning as a method of travel.

I have often seen and collected them from the surface of the snow, even on days when the temperature was below freezing.

Description: Female's body is 2 to 3 mm long. Male's is 1 to 2 mm. Legspans range from 5 to 6 mm.

Abdomen: Gray to dark. Rounded with a posterior point. Spinnerets are visible.

Carapace: Light brown to nearly black. Head is held high; especially the male's. Row of small teeth-like bumps on lateral edges.

Legs: Brown and uniformly colored.

Chelicerae: Jaws have five to seven teeth.

Hunting Technique: Capture tiny fauna in tiny sheet webs.

Web: Small sheet webs near the ground.

Egg Sac & Eggs: Egg sac is hidden near the ground.

Life Cycle: Mating takes place in early summer. Overwinter in various stages of growth.

Splendid Dwarf Spider   *Hypselistes florens*

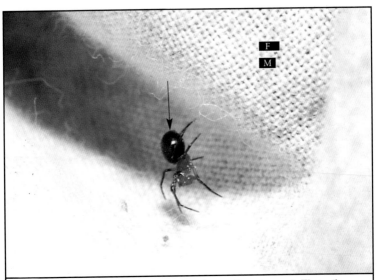

Under dead leaves, rocks and debris on the ground. Though common, they are usually not seen.

Description: Female's body is 2 to 3 mm long. Male's is 2 to 3 mm. Legspans range from 5 to 6 mm.

Abdomen: Black and spherical ↑. Covered with a hard shiny plate.

Carapace: Red and flat, but with a pronounced head and face.

Eyes: Two AME are above the other six eyes.

Legs: Top is reddish, similar to the carapace. Lower part is gray. Medium-length with spines.

Chelicerae: Jaws have many teeth.

Hunting Technique: Capture tiny fauna in tiny sheet webs.

Web: Tiny sheet webs near the ground.

Egg Sac & Eggs: Egg sac is hidden near the ground.

Life Cycle: Males mature earlier in summer than females. Overwinter as penultimate.

Nature Notes:

Tiny spiders are often ballooners. Even adult *Hypselistes* use this technique to get around.

I have often seen and collected these spiders on the surface of the snow; even during January and February.

Splendid Dwarf Spiders are occasionally found on the snow's surface; even in mid-winter.

Orbweavers
Family Araneidae

Araneids are best known by the orb webs they construct; sometimes very large and mostly made on summer nights. Diverse in shape and color, they typically have a small face and small eyes with a large abdomen.

Description

A large and very diverse family. Small to large spiders (5 to 25 mm). Females are much larger than males.

Abdomen: Large and rounded with spots, lines or zigzag patterns. Some have spines or humps. Many show a folium pattern.

Carapace: Much smaller than the abdomen and usually uniformly-colored with few if any patterns.

Eyes: Eight small eyes in two rows. Lateral eyes may be separated from median eyes.

Legs: Short and spiny. Pairs one and two project forward while pairs three and four point backward. Three claws.

Chelicerae: Not large.

Similar Spiders

Tetragnathids (long-jawed orbweavers) also make orb webs, but they are much thinner with longer legs and long chelicerae (jaws).

Habitat

In such a big family there is bound to be diversity in habitat preferences. Orbweavers may be found in grasses, shrubs, trees, woods, caves and human-made sites (cabins, garages, outhouses, fences, signs and porches).

Hunting Technique

With poor vision, the sedentary orbweavers must sit in, or near, the web and feel their captives as they struggle in the threads. Prey is held and turned by the front legs, while rear legs wrap the victim with silk. Food is often carried to the retreat to be eaten. Many build a new web each evening and hunt at night. Others are diurnal.

Web

The hunting snare is a circular web known as an orb. Web placement is usually vertical with a nearby retreat. The hub is closed, and some construct a zigzag stabilimentum in the center (*Argiope* spiders). Threads called spokes, or radii, go from the outer edge to the center. These threads are not sticky. Circular threads winding to the center are sticky. Spider waits inverted on the hub or in the retreat.

Observations

Since web-builders are nearly blind, males must use a series of web vibrations to court and approach the female on her web lest they be confused for prey.

Egg Sac & Eggs

Egg sac is spherical and attached to nearby plants or the spider's retreat. Some hatch in late summer or fall, others in spring. Spiderlings balloon upon dispersal.

**orb-style web;
note closed hub**

Diversity

About 200 species are found in North America. Ten genera in this guide.

Acanthepeira	*Cyclosa*	*Neoscona*
Araneus	*Eustala*	*Lariniodes (Nuctenea)*
Araniella	*Hypsosinga*	
Argiope	*Mangora*	

Orbweavers (Family Araneidae)

64 Star-bellied Orbweaver (*Acanthepeira*)
66 Shamrock Orbweaver (*Araneus*)
68 Marbled Orbweaver (*Araneus*)
70 Nordman's Orbweaver (*Araneus*)
72 Cross Orbweaver (*Araneus*)
74 Six-spotted Orbweaver (*Araniella*)
76 Yellow Garden Argiope (*Argiope*)
78 Banded Argiope (*Argiope*)
80 Cone-shaped Orbweaver (*Cyclosa*)
82 Hump-backed Orbweaver (*Eustala*)
84 Pygmy Variable Orbweaver (*Hypsosinga*)
85 Tuft-legged Orbweaver (*Mangora*)
86 Arabesque Orbweaver (*Neoscona*)
88 Furrow Spider (*Lariniodes*)

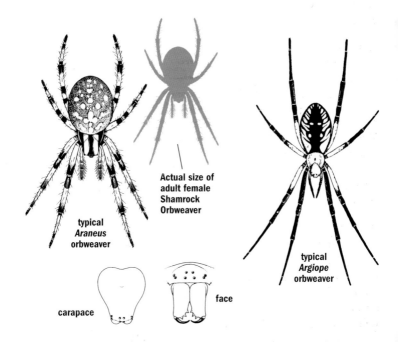

**Actual size of
adult female
Shamrock
Orbweaver**

**typical
Araneus
orbweaver**

**typical
Argiope
orbweaver**

carapace

face

Star-bellied Orbweaver *Acanthepeira stellata*

F
M

Fields, meadows and woodland edges. Tall grasses and low bushes.

Nature Notes:

When I find the webs it is usually early in the morning when dew-covered; the spider patiently sitting in the hub.

A regular, but not abundant, part of the meadow fauna.

Description: Female's body is 10 to 12 mm long. Male's is 6 to 7 mm. Legspans range from 9 to 15 mm.

Abdomen: Dramatic. Outer edge sports twelve cone-shaped projections. Middle front cone overhangs the carapace. Rear cone overhangs the spinnerets. Four to five cones on each side. Brown with light patterns on anterior part.

Carapace: Insignificant compared to the large abdomen. Mostly flat and dark brown. Head is high and set off by a well-marked cervical groove from the thorax.

Legs: Short and yellowish; ringed with brown.

Hunting Technique: With poor vision, they must sit in, or near, the web and feel their captives as they struggle in the threads. Prey is held and turned by the front legs, while rear legs wrap the victim with silk. Food is often carried to the retreat to be eaten.

Star-bellied Orbweavers have the large abdomen and small carapace typical of members of the family Araneidae.

You can find Star-bellied Orbweavers in the middle of their 6 to 10-inch diameter orb webs even on dewy mornings.

Web: Vertical orb webs, 6 to 10 inches in diameter with about 25 radii, built on the upper half of vegetation. The spider may sit in the hub, but usually can be found in the retreat.

Egg Sac & Eggs: Egg sac is attached to leaves near the web.

Life Cycle: Males mature in spring; females in summer. Adults can be found all summer and into the fall. Overwinter in penultimate or immature instar.

Spiny projections on the abdomen make this orbweaver unmistakable.

Shamrock Orbweaver   *Araneus trifolium*

Woodlands, gardens, fences, bridges and eaves of buildings.
Webs built in tall grass, shrubs and among tree branches.

Nature Notes:

The Shamrock
Orbweaver is probably
the spider most often
associated with large,
circular orb webs.

Females, with their huge
abdomens, are conspicu-
ous in late summer and
early fall.

Over 1500 species
worldwide in this genus!

Description: Female's body is 6 to 20 mm
long. Male's is 5 to 13 mm. Legspans range
from 20 to 40 mm.

Abdomen: Large. Can be pale green, brown,
gray or reddish. Large and small pale spots.
Background is evenly colored.

Carapace: Central black stripe ↑ bordered by
two light and two black side stripes.

Legs: Striking black-and-white striped legs ↑.
Medium to long.

Hunting Technique: With poor vision, orbweavers must sit in, or near, the web and feel
their captives as they struggle in the threads.
Prey is held and turned by the front legs, while
rear legs wrap the victim with silk. Food is often
carried to the retreat to be eaten.

Web: Vertical orbs, 20 to 30 inches in diameter
with 15 to 35 radii. Closed hub. Many make a
retreat out of a rolled up leaf or silk. It is near

Shamrock Orbweavers can be dramatically colored as in the photo on the right, or pale, as pictured above left. They always show the large-spotted abdomen and wide black rings on the legs.

the web and attached by signal lines. Spiders are often in their retreat but sometimes in the center of the web. Typically, each night the old web is replaced with a new one.

Egg Sac & Eggs: Eggs are laid and the sacs made in summer and fall.

Life Cycle: Adults mature in mid summer. Females may remain active until mid autumn, but males are found only during the brief period of maturity. Egg sacs are made in summer and fall. They overwinter in sacs as eggs or young; dispersing in the spring.

This is the typical snare of the *Araneus* orbweavers.

Marbled Orbweaver   *Araneus marmoreus*

| F | |
| M | |

Woodlands, gardens, fences, bridges and eaves of buildings. Webs built in tall grass, shrubs and among tree branches.

Nature Notes:

Marbled Orbweavers, and other orbweavers, construct a tubular silk retreat near the web. From the relative security of the retreat, they can monitor the web for vibrations. Prey is also brought here to eat.

Araneus spiders are probably those most often associated with large, circular orb webs.

Description: Female's body is 9 to 18 mm long. Male's is 6 to 9 mm. Legspans range from 18 to 36 mm.

Abdomen: Rounded with no caudal humps. Colors vary widely; from orange to brownish to purple to pink. Markings create a "marbled" appearance ↑ along the front and sides. Scalloped folium may be inconspicuous.

Carapace: Yellow with darker lines on side and middle. Brown sternum.

Legs: Medium to long, and ringed. Red femur ↑.

Hunting Technique: With poor vision, orb-weavers must sit in, or near, the web and feel their captives as they struggle in the threads. Prey is held and turned by the front legs, while rear legs wrap the victim with silk. Food is often carried to the retreat to be eaten.

Marbled Orbweavers come in a wide variety of colors and patterns. This beauty was silver, black and pink in her prime, but faded to a pale orange and gray in autumn. Here she sits in her woven silk retreat waiting for the telltale vibrations from her nearby orb web. (Note marbling on front edge of abdomen.)

Web: Vertical orbs, 20 to 30 inches in diameter with 15 to 35 radii. Closed hub. Many make a retreat out of a rolled up leaf or silk. It is near the web and attached by signal lines. Spiders are often in their retreat but sometimes in the center of the web. Typically, each night the old web is replaced with a new one.

Egg Sac & Eggs: Egg sacs are made in summer and fall.

Life Cycle: Adults mature in mid summer. Females may remain active until mid autumn, but males are found only during the brief period of maturity. Egg sacs are made in summer and fall. They overwinter in sacs as eggs or young, dispersing in the spring.

Colors of the Marbled Orbweavers vary, but they will always show the marbling effect on the front of the abdomen.

Nordman's Orbweaver   probably *Araneus nordmanni*

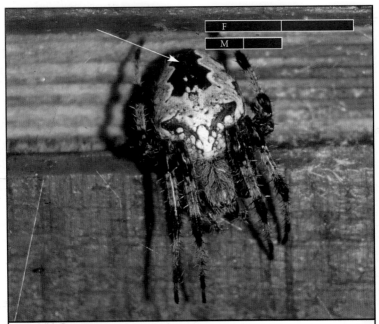

	F	
	M	

Dense woodlands. Webs built in tall grass, shrubs, among tree branches and under eaves of buildings.

Description: Female's body is 7 to 19 mm long. Male's is 5 to 10 mm. Legspans range from 20 to 40 mm.

Abdomen: Slight shoulder humps. Black, brown and green. Pointed terminal end. Folium can be solid black posteriorly ↑ with a white border. Variable.

Carapace: Covered in hairs. Even-colored.

Legs: Long and ringed.

Hunting Technique: With poor vision, orb-weavers must sit in, or near, the web and feel their captives as they struggle in the threads. Prey is held and turned by the front legs, while rear legs wrap the victim with silk. Food is often carried to a retreat to be eaten.

This orbweaver hangs upside-down in its protected web under the eaves of a cabin.

Web: Vertical orbs with a closed hub. Many make a retreat out of a rolled up leaf or silk. It is near the web and attached by signal lines. Spiders are often in their retreat but sometimes in the center of the web. Typically, each night the old web is replaced with a new one.

Egg Sac & Eggs: Egg sacs are made in summer and fall.

Life Cycle: Adults mature in mid to late summer. Females may remain active until mid autumn, but males are found only during the brief period of maturity. Egg sacs are made in summer and fall. They overwinter in sacs as eggs or young, dispersing in the spring.

Cross Orbweaver   possibly *Araneus diadematus*

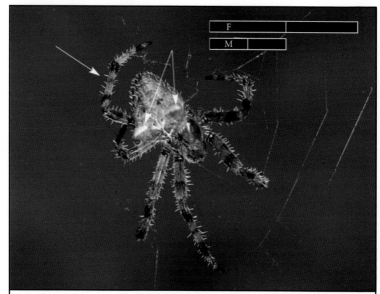

F	
M	

Woodlands, gardens, fences, bridges and eaves of buildings.
Webs built in tall grass, shrubs, tree branches and buildings.

Nature Notes:

The spider pictured above could very well be another species of humped orb-weaver. Identification of *Araneus* spiders, to species, is surprisingly difficult. Abdomen colors and patterns can vary dramatically even within a species. As with many spiders, exact IDs often come down to differences in microscopic body parts.

The Cross Orbweaver is common throughout the northern hemisphere. It has been studied extensively in Europe.

Description: Female's body is 7 to 20 mm long. Male's is 5 to 13 mm. Legspans range from 20 to 40 mm.

Abdomen: Pronounced shoulder humps ↑ at widest point anteriorly. Light brown. Folium is usually fairly indistinct but will show some black spots ↑. On darker specimens, a white cross-shape can be formed near the carapace.

Carapace: Dark median stripe and side stripes.

Legs: Long and quite spiny ↑. Ringed.

Hunting Technique: Cross Orbweavers will sit in their orb web all day; only retreating during bad weather.

Web: Vertical orbs with a closed hub. Many make a retreat out of a rolled up leaf or silk. It is near the web and attached by signal lines. Spiders are often in their retreat but sometimes in the center of the web. Typically, each night the old web is replaced with a new one.

Another very common late summer humped orbweaver is this species. It may be *Araneus gemmoides*.

Egg Sac & Eggs: Female leaves web to deposit eggs under loose bark and in crevices.

Life Cycle: Adults mature in mid to late summer. Females may remain active until mid autumn, but males are found only during the brief period of maturity. They overwinter as eggs or young; dispersing in the spring.

Six-spotted Orbweaver   *Araniella displicata*

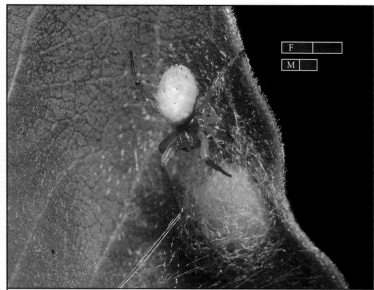

Meadows, fields and pastures. Tall grasses and bushes. Often on broadleaf trees and shrubs.

Nature Notes:

When the snow is deep, more young survive to disperse in early summer.

Description: Female's body is 5 to 9 mm long. Male's is 4 to 6 mm. Legspans range from 10 to 17 mm.

Abdomen: Oval with no folium patterns. Yellow, white or pinkish with three pairs of tiny black spots ↑ on the posterior half.

Carapace: Yellow to brown without markings and darker than the abdomen. Smooth with almost no setae and no thoracic depressions.

Eyes: On black spots.

Legs: Yellow to brown with spines. Legs longer in males than female.

Hunting Technique: With poor vision, orb-weavers must sit in, or near, the web and feel their captives as they struggle in the threads. Prey is held and turned by the front legs, while rear legs wrap the victim with silk.

A Horse Fly falls prey to the much smaller Six-spotted Orbweaver. As in many spiders, a sticky web and potent venom allows them to take prey much larger than themselves.

Web: Orb in tall grasses and bushes but nearer the ground. Small web, often in the space enclosed by the bending of a single large leaf. No retreat; spider stays at the hub.

Egg Sac & Eggs: Egg sacs made in summer. It is wrapped in golden silk and attached to a leaf. Sacs are guarded by the female (see photo on left hand page).

Life Cycle: Overwinters in penultimate and other young instars. Matures in spring. Mating takes place in spring and early summer with egg sacs in summer.

Yellow Garden Argiope *Argiope aurantia*

Gardens, fields, roadsides, yards and near houses. Tall grasses and weeds in open areas. Shrubs and flowers of meadows.

Nature Notes:

Probably the largest web-building spider in the North.

More common at the southern edge of the North Woods.

Males are much smaller than females; often only a quarter her size!

The relatively tiny male may build a web in the outlying part of a female's web.

Description: Female's body is 19 to 28 mm long. Male's is 5 to 8 mm. Legspans range from 18 to 70 mm.

Abdomen: Ovoid with pairs of basal humps. Median dorsal area is black, sides are marked with large yellow bands separated by narrow black stripes that connect to the black median.

Carapace: Gray and yellow carapace is hidden by a dense covering of silvery pubescence. Black sternum with a yellow median stripe.

Legs: Front legs are nearly all black; sometimes with a narrow orange band on the femur. All other legs are black with a yellow or red femur.

Hunting Technique: Spider sits inverted in the center of the web waiting for large flying insects to be snared.

Web: Huge orb web constructed in a sunny location. May be three feet or more in diameter

Recent research has found evidence that the zigzag stabilimentum may reflect ultraviolet light and thereby attract insects. It also helps to camouflage the spider as it sits in the hub.

with 30 to 50 radii. Zigzag stabilimentum ↑ in center. No retreat.

Egg Sac & Eggs: Egg sacs are produced in late summer and fall. The sac is attached to vegetation near the web. More than one thousand eggs may occupy a single sac!

Life Cycle: Spiders mature in late summer. Egg sacs are produced in late summer and fall. Spiderlings overwinter inside the cocoon. Young disperse in the spring.

Banded Argiope *Argiope trifasciata*

Gardens, fields, roadsides, yards and near houses. Webs made in tall grasses, shrubs and weeds in meadows.

Nature Notes:

I once saw over 100 dew-covered Banded Argiopes in their webs in a single field. It was a mid-September day and a week later they were all gone.

The relatively tiny male may build a web in the outlying part of the female's web.

The Banded Argiope is more common in the North Woods than its close cousin, the Yellow Garden Argiope.

Description: Female's body is 15 to 25 mm long. Male's is 4 to 6 mm. Legspans range from 15 to 60 mm.

Abdomen: More pointed than in Yellow Garden Argiope but with no basal humps. A beautiful and striking pattern of alternating silver, yellow and black bands ↑. Venter: Black with yellow longitudinal bands and red spinnerets ↑.

Carapace: Gray and yellow carapace is hidden by a dense covering of silvery pubescence. Black sternum with a yellow stripe.

Legs: Narrow rings of orange and black ↑.

Hunting Technique: Spider sits inverted in center of web waiting for large flying insects to be trapped.

Web: Huge orb web constructed in a sunny location. May be three feet or more in diameter.

Argiope spiders hang inverted in the web waiting to feel the vibrations of caught prey. Their legs overlap so they appear as a large "X" in the middle of the web.

30 to 50 radii. Center zigzag stabilimentum may be incorporated into the web. No retreat is built.

Egg Sac & Eggs: Egg sacs are produced in late summer and fall. The sac is attached to vegetation near the web. More than one thousand eggs may occupy a single sac!

Life Cycle: Spiders mature in late summer. Egg sacs are produced in late summer and fall. Spiderlings overwinter inside the cocoon. Young disperse in the spring.

A grasshopper is wrapped in silk for later consumption. Banded Argiope regularly take prey twice their own body length.

Cone-shaped Orbweaver   *Cyclosa conica*

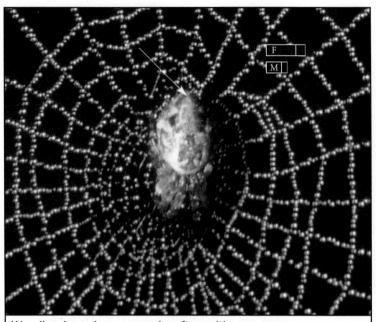

Woodlands and open woods; often with evergreens.

Nature Notes:

Webs of *Cyclosa* are unique in that the spiral goes all the way to the center without a gap or "free zone."

One of the smallest orbweavers in the North Woods.

Description: Female's body is 5 to 7.5 mm long. Male's is 3 to 4 mm. Legspans range from 6 to 11 mm.

Abdomen: Long caudal hump that varies in different individuals, but often extends beyond the spinnerets and looks like a cone ↑. This trait gives this spider its common name. Varied pattern of dark and light colors.

Carapace: Mixture of gray and white to almost all black. Carapace is usually covered by the legs when it is sitting in the web.

Eyes: Located on prominent tubercles.

Legs: Pale brown.

Males are similar to females, but usually more subdued in color and with a shorter caudal hump.

Cyclosa orbweavers are much smaller than their cousins, the *Araneus* and *Argiope* orb-weavers, but their snares, whose threads spiral all the way to the middle, are easy to identify.

Hunting Technique: Like most orbweavers, they sit inverted in the middle of their web until they feel vibrations from trapped prey. These spiders drop to the ground when disturbed.

Web: Orb web with many spokes (30-50 radii). Spirals go to, or very near the hub. Often with a short stabilimentum in the center. Web may be wider than tall and about six feet off the ground. No retreat is built.

Egg Sac & Eggs: Egg sac placed near the web in twigs and leaves.

Life Cycle: Males mature in spring; females in early summer. Adults are around all summer. Overwinter as penultimate or other immature instars.

Hump-backed Orbweaver   *Eustala anastera*

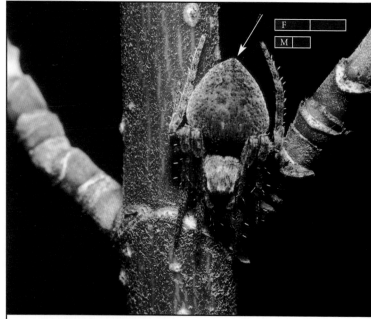

Bushes, shrubs and low trees; often near water.

Description: Female's body is 6 to 10 mm long. Male's is 4 to 6 mm. Legspans range from 10 to 20 mm.

Abdomen: Front half is wider than the bluntly pointed end ↑. Hump above the spinnerets is most apparent when viewed from the side. Mostly gray with a central scallop-edged diamond stretching from the anterior end to the posterior. This folium mark may be very faint.

Carapace: Light to medium gray; darker on the sides.

Legs: Mostly gray with irregular rings. Spined.

Hunting Technique: Spider often sits off to the side with leg touching the web; waiting for vibrations from potential victims.

Web: Orb webs are built in the evening in upper portions of a plant and removed by morning.

Nature Notes:

One of the few orb-weavers to overwinter in penultimate stage.

I have found the Hump-backed Orbweaver earlier in the summer than other orbweavers.

Ahh, the life of a spider! Just hanging out and fishing. Actually this orbweaver has one web line attached to its raised leg to feel for struggling prey. Web-building spiders have poor vision so they must rely on these vibrations.

Egg Sac & Eggs: Eggs are produced in the summer.

Life Cycle: Matures in the middle of spring to early summer. Adult males and females may be found all summer. Mating and eggs occur in the summer. Overwinters in penultimate stage.

When the Hump-backed Orbweaver is in the web, the legs are spread wide to contact the maximum number of threads and feel for the slightest disturbance.

Pygmy Variable Orbweaver   *Hypsosinga variabilis*

Meadows and fields. Low vegetation in damp places.

Nature Notes:

This species is sometimes called *Singa pygmaea*. The "pygmy" reference relates to its diminutive size.

Most likely our only striped orbweaver.

Description: Female's body is 3 to 4 mm long. Male's is 2.5 mm. Legspans range from 4 to 6 mm.

Abdomen: Black with three light stripes ↑; medium one is yellow. Side stripes don't wrap all the way around to front. But as the Latin name implies, the abdomen pattern can be quite variable. Appears shiny.

Carapace: Light orange with black around the ocular region.

Legs: Short and orange without markings.

Hunting Technique: Sit and wait for prey in the web.

Web: A small orb.

Egg Sac & Eggs: Eggs found in summer.

Life Cycle: Overwinters as half-grown spider and matures in spring. Eggs found in summer.

Tuft-legged Orbweaver   *Mangora placida*

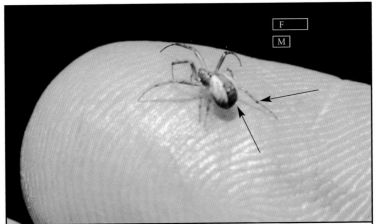

Bushes and trees in forested areas. Low bushes and tall grass in meadows.

Description: Female's body is 2.5 to 4.5 mm long. Male's is 2 to 2.8 mm. Legspans range from 5 to 10 mm.

Abdomen: Elliptical and a bit wider behind the middle. Yellow-white patches on either side of a wide dark-brown median stripe ↑; black sides.

Carapace: Yellow with brown stripes down the middle and along each side.

Legs: Yellow with fairly long spines and a tuft of hairs on the tibia ↑.

Hunting Technique: Spider rests in the hub or in a curled leaf above the fine-mesh web.

Web: A delicate and beautiful snare. Orb with many radii (30 to 70) and close spirals. The web appears to be an intricate structure of fine lace. Web is about twelve inches across; vertical or inclined towards the horizontal.

Egg Sac & Eggs: Egg sac is produced in early fall and hidden in small, folded leaves.

Life Cycle: Spiders mature in spring with adults found throughout the summer. Egg sac is produced in early fall. Young hatch in the fall, but stay with eggs until spring. Overwinter as immatures.

Nature Notes:

One of the smallest of our orb-weaving spiders.

An intricate orb web with numerous radii and many spirals is a sure sign that this spider is present.

This tiny orbweaver looks more like a member of the Theridiidae; the cobweb weavers.

Young may disperse by ballooning.

Arabesque Orbweaver *Neoscona arabesca*

F

M

Sunny moist sites. Tall grasses and low bushes in fields. Edges of woods or open woods.

Nature Notes:

A common genus of orb-weaving spiders. Often found in vegetation near homes.

Unique habit of sitting in the hub of its web with the tip of the abdomen pushed through an open space.

Description: Female's body is 5 to 12 mm long. Male's is 4 to 9 mm. Legspans range from 18 to 30 mm.

Abdomen: Oval to triangular; higher near the anterior end. Yellow and brown with five pairs of slanted black dashes ↑ on posterior half. Black venter framed by angular white marks.

Carapace: Gray with brown median band. Submarginal brown lines on sides. Longitudinal thoracic groove.

Legs: Pale with brown bands ↑. Spined.

Hunting Technique: Spider sits in hub with tip of abdomen pushed through an open space. Usually no retreat is used. If disturbed, the spider goes quickly to a twig or grass stalk near the web.

Web: An orb, six to eighteen inches across, placed vertically in grasses or low bushes. About 20 radii.

Neoscona arabesca is an orbweaver that has a showy yellow and brown abdomen, red and black striped legs and four pairs of slanting black abdominal marks.

Egg Sac & Eggs: Produced in late summer.

Life Cycle: Males mature in early summer; females later. Egg sacs are produced in late summer. Overwinter as eggs.

Furrow Spider *Larinioides cornuta* (formerly *Nuctenea c.*)

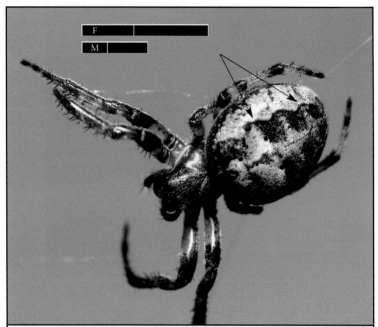

Low bushes near water. Often around houses; under eaves and porches. Also fences and bridge railings.

Nature Notes:

Larinioides (Nuctenea) are best identified by the cross on the back and the light parenthesis marks on their undersides. Both are visible as they sit in their vertical orb web.

Genus *Nuctenea* was recently split into two genera. Our species are in *Larinioides*. *Nuctenea* now only refers to a few palearctic species.

A common orbweaver of late summer.

Description: Female's body is 6 to 14 mm long. Male's is 5 to 9 mm. Legspans range from 18 to 35 mm.

Abdomen: Flattened on the posterior part. Folium is grayish brown and outlined in black; usually with unbroken zigzag edges ↑. Light pattern in middle of folium usually cross-shaped. Background is light or dark; often reddish brown. Male is more gray. Venter is dark brown with a pair of lateral yellowish lines that curve towards each other at the posterior end; they resemble yellow parenthesis ↑.

Carapace: Gray, olive or brown.

Legs: Spiny with dark rings.

Hunting Technique: The spider sits inverted in the center of the web or in the retreat at the end of a radius thread.

On the Furrow Spider's undersides note the yellow parenthesis-shaped marks that terminate near the spinnerets. This field mark is easy to see on spiders that are hanging in the middle of their webs.

Web: Vertical orb with usually less than 20 radii and widely spaced spirals. Webs are spun in the evening.

Egg Sac & Eggs: Egg sacs are produced in spring to midsummer and hidden in the retreat.

Life Cycle: Adult males and females occur throughout the year. Spiders may live for a couple years. Mature in spring. Egg sacs are produced in spring to midsummer and hidden in the retreat. Females and males may occupy the same web.

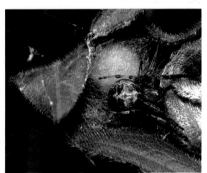

Egg sacs are made in midsummer and placed in the retreat made of folded leaves.

Long-jawed Orbweavers Family Tetragnathidae

Tetragnathids may be best known as the long, thin spiders that make orb webs on the shores of wet areas; ponds, swamps, lakes and rivers.

Description

Large but slender spiders with long legs. Body sizes range from 6 to 13 mm.

Abdomen: Much longer than wide; brown, gray, cream, whitish or green. Sometimes with a stripe or other subtle patterns.

Carapace: Longer than wide. Usually light-colored.

Eyes: Two rows of equally-sized eyes; parallel or nearly so. Lateral eyes are separated from medial eyes.

Legs: Very long except for the third pair. Mostly with short spines and three claws. The first and second pair of legs extend forward, third pair straight out to the sides and the fourth pair towards the rear.

Chelicerae: Huge jaw parts–often as long as the carapace–give this family its common name.

Similar Spiders

Linyphiids (sheetweb weavers) can also be thin, but lack the huge chelicerae and spin sheet webs. Araneids (orbweavers) spin a similar web but with a closed hub. Araneids also have a much wider, rounded abdomen.

Habitat

Long-jawed orbweavers are common in tall vegetation near water; marshes, swamps, ponds, lakes and even bogs. Some species can be found away from water in meadows. They spin orb webs in the evening which become obvious in the dew of morning.

Hunting Technique

Spiders sit in the center of the web or cling to a nearby stalk. With their thin bodies stretched out along the stalk, they virtually disappear.

Web

Tetragnathids produce orb webs that are usually at an angle between vertical and horizontal. Webs have relatively few radii (12 to 20), widely spaced spirals and an open hub.

Observations

Anyone who has ever gone wild ricing knows the members of this family well. The rice is knocked into the canoe along with hundreds of these spiders.

Egg Sac & Eggs

The egg sac is attached to twigs and covered with threads.

Diversity
About 25 species are found in North America. Three genera in this guide.

> *Leucauge*
> *Pachygnatha*
> *Tetragnatha*

Long-jawed Orbweavers (Family Tetragnathidae)

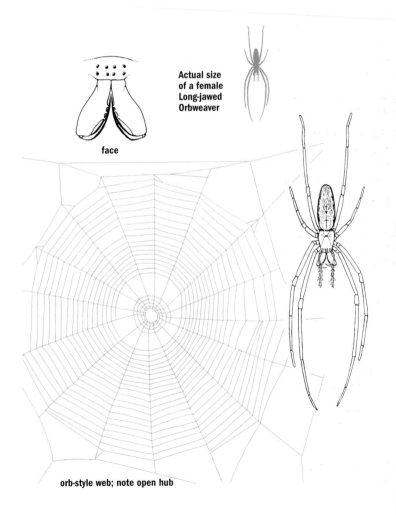

face

Actual size
of a female
Long-jawed
Orbweaver

orb-style web; note open hub

Orchard Orbweaver   *Leucauge venusta*

Densely wooded areas, woodland edges and shrubby meadows. Webs in low bushes and trees.

Description: Female's body is 5 to 8 mm long. Male's is 3 to 4 mm. Legspans range from 10 to 22 mm.

Abdomen: Striking pattern; shiny silver above with dark stripes. Sides yellow with red spots near the caudal end. Red spots underneath ↑ that seem to glow from the shadows. Caudal end is black. Elliptically bulbous with a pointed end underneath. Longer than wide.

Carapace: Longer than wide. Yellowish green-gray striped with brown on the sides.

Legs: Thin and fairly long; first pair is longest. Long, feathery trichobothria hairs on hind femur.

Hunting Technique: Spider clings inverted to the underside center of the web, often with the abdomen directly under the open hub.

Web: Orb web can be horizontal to near-vertical or any angle in between. About twelve inches in diameter with about 30 radii. Webs are usually in

Nature Notes:

Fairly unusual in the North Woods but they have been recorded on a northern Lake Michigan island.

Probably the most arboreal of the Tetragnathids.

More common in the south. Found all the way down to the Florida Keys.

The two red spots on the Orchard Orbweaver's undersides seem to glow from its haunts in dark forests.

wooded areas with a subcanopy of shrubs and trees. Open hub with irregular barrier webs below.

Egg Sac & Eggs: Egg sac attached to leaves and twigs near the web.

Life Cycle: Males mature in early summer; females shortly thereafter. Spiderlings disperse and spin their own webs. Overwinter as an immature.

The Orchard Orbweaver is easily disturbed and will drop immediately to the ground to avoid detection.

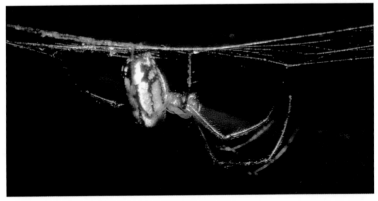

Three-striped Thick-jawed Orbweaver

Pachygnatha tristriata

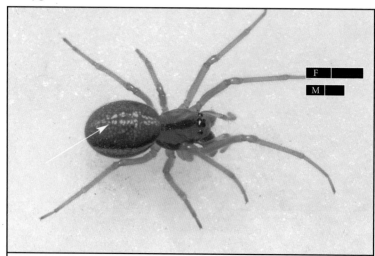

Found on the ground under stones and leaves. Often near water. Occasionally in grasslands. Rarely seen in the web.

Nature Notes:

The only orbweaver that usually does not make a web.

Frequently found in meadows in late summer.

I have even photographed them on snow in early winter (see photos above).

Description: Female's body is 6 to 7 mm long. Male's is 5 to 6 mm. Legspans range from 10 to 15 mm.

Abdomen: Oval and rounded. Two light center stripes made up of spots and dashes ↑. Black stripes bordering the silver and gray along the sides.

Carapace: Oval and flattened. Dark with a few light markings.

Eyes: Ocular region is above the carapace.

Legs: Pale and uniformly yellow.

Chelicerae: Powerful, thick and divergent.

Hunting Technique: Wander in search of small insect prey.

Web: Young construct small horizontal orb webs near the ground. Adults do not make webs.

This adult Three-striped Thick-jawed Orbweaver is out for a midwinter stroll. Its presence is good evidence that at least some overwinter as adults.

Egg Sac & Eggs: The egg sac is attached to twigs and covered with threads.

Life Cycle: Matures and immatures are found in summer. They have been collected on the surface of the snow in early winter. They may overwinter as adults.

Young *Pachygnatha* spiders make small horizontal orb webs near the ground as this unidentified species has done. Adults do not make webs at all; they actively hunt.

Long-jawed Orbweaver sp. *Tetragnatha* species

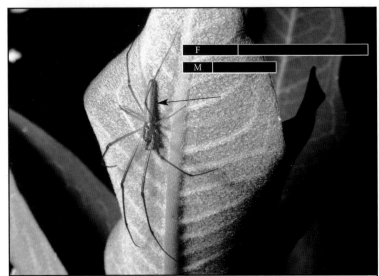

Marshes, meadows, shrubby wet areas and wild rice beds.
Webs built in branches, dry grasses, cattails and sedges near water.

Nature Notes:

Spiders often hide by stretching out along a twig or grass blade and hold on with the third pair of legs.

Webs are very common on dead branches in swamps; some may be very high off the ground. Spiders frequently live on shoreline plants. They are often knocked into passing boats.

This is the genus of spider that appears to make the wild rice in the bottom of your ricing canoe crawl. As the wild rice is bent over the gunnels and the rice heads knocked into the canoe, these spiders fall in too.

Description: Female's body is 5 to 15 mm long. Male's is 4 to 8 mm. Legspans range from 25 to 50 mm.

Abdomen: Long and narrow ↑; may be wider near the base. Brown-gray with central dark bands that may be vein-like. Some are silvery or silver-striped on the sides. Undersides may be dark to light brown.

Carapace: Reddish brown, yellow or tan.

Legs: Very long and slender. First, second and fourth pair are all twice the length of the body.

Chelicerae: Long; almost as long as the carapace in some species. Some jaws are divergent while others are more vertical. All have many teeth.

Hunting Technique: Spiders sit in the center of the web or cling to a nearby stalk. With their thin bodies stretched out, they blend in well.

Web: Orb with an open hub built in meadows and marshes near open water. Web is often inclined, some may be nearly horizontal. Twelve to 20 radii with widely spaced spirals. No retreat is made or used. Web is built new

Long-jawed orbweavers construct their snares in tall grasses near lakes, rivers and marshes. This spider moved quickly as it constructed its orb web at sunset.

each night. Spiders are most active as dusk; especially in warm and calm weather. Spider may rest in the hub or along the edge of the web.

Egg Sac & Eggs: Egg sacs are produced in summer and placed on twigs. They are not guarded.

Life Cycle: Spiders mature in spring to late summer. Spiderlings quickly disperse and make webs of their own. Young will balloon. May overwinter as immatures.

There are at least 17 species of *Tetragnatha* in the United States.
A few North Woods varieties are pictured below. Note the similarities in body structure.

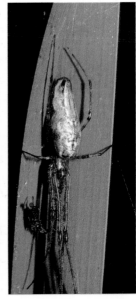

Green Long-jawed Orbweaver *Tetragnatha viridis*

Pine woodlands near water. Black spruce bogs.

Nature Notes:

At first glance, the Green Long-jawed Orbweaver does not appear to be a Tetragnathid. But upon close inspection we can see the longer jaws and tubular abdomen–characteristics of this family.

I have seen this spider on the snow during mild winter days.

Found from Florida to the Boundary Waters Canoe Area. It is a widespread species.

Description: Female's body is 5 to 7 mm long. Male's is 4 to 7 mm. Legspans range from 10 to 15 mm.

Abdomen: Green and long ↑; orangish marks ↑ at anterior end. Faint mottled-silver stripes.

Carapace: Bright lime green.

Legs: Green, long and slender. First, second and fourth pair are all twice the length of the body.

Chelicerae: Long, but not as long as in other species.

Eyes: Both rows of similarly-sized small eyes are easily visible on the green face.

Hunting Technique: Spiders sit in the center of the web or cling to a nearby stalk. With their thin bodies stretched out, they blend in well with the twigs or stalks.

Web: Orb with an open hub built near water. Web is often inclined, some may be nearly horizontal. No retreat is made or used. Web is built new each night. Spiders are most active as dusk;

Green Long-jawed Orbweavers are much smaller than some of their *Tetragnatha* cousins. Watch for them in areas of pines near water. For size comparison, note the pine needles in this photo.

especially in warm and calm weather. Spider may rest in the hub or along the edge of the web.

Egg Sac & Eggs: Egg sacs are produced in summer and placed on twigs. They are not guarded.

Life Cycle: Spiders mature in spring to late summer. Spiderlings quickly disperse and make webs of their own. Young will balloon. May overwinter as immatures.

If you look carefully on mild winter days in the North, you can see all kinds of spiders out and about.

Nursery Web Spiders
Family Pisauridae

Pisaurids are probably best known as the large spiders that run over the water's surface along the margins of ponds, swamps and lakes. They also climb up onto nearby shores, docks and cabins. Commonly called "fishing spiders".

Description

Large spiders (15 to 25 mm). Members of this family have the longest legspan of any spider in the North Woods.

Abdomen: Ovoid with short hairs. Brown and gray with stripes, spots or other markings. Female is nearly twice the size of the male.

Carapace: Longer than wide and flattened. Brown or gray with stripes.

Eyes: Posterior medial eyes (PME) are slightly larger than others. Anterior row is straight to recurved; posterior row is strongly recurved. Good eyesight. Eyes possess tapetum layer that reflects light, creating a green eyeshine at night.

Legs: Long. First two pairs are usually held together. All legs nearly equal in length with three claws.

Chelicerae: Large and powerful; three to four teeth.

Similar Spiders

Lycosids (wolf spiders) may look similar but have different patterns on the carapace and abdomen and have huge posterior median eyes (PME). Nursery web spiders are usually found near water.

Habitat

Usually found on or near permanent bodies of water: ponds, swamps, lakes and slow-moving rivers. Also seen on docks and cabins near the water. When on the water's surface, they are usually among aquatic vegetation. Some also found in grassy meadows. *Dolomedes tenebrosus* wanders far from water.

Hunting Technique

Spiders sit quietly for hours with legs spread wide. They hunt by placing tips of legs on the water's surface as they sit on nearby substrate. Spiders are semi-aquatic and can stay underwater for as long as thirty minutes. Here they feed on insects, tadpoles and even small fish (giving them the name of fishing spiders). With good vision, they can hunt day or night.

Web

No snare is spun for catching prey, but females do sew leaves together to create nursery webs.

Observations
Male brings a fly to the female when courting. Young hatch in mid summer and leave the nursery web after about a week.

Egg Sac & Eggs
Large spherical egg sac is constructed and carried by the female. It is held in the jaws with a few silk strands connecting it to the spinnerets as well. Wolf spiders attach their sacs only to the spinnerets.

Diversity
About 15 species are found in North America. Two genera in this guide.

> *Dolomedes*
> *Pisaurina*

Nursery Web Spiders (Family Pisauridae)

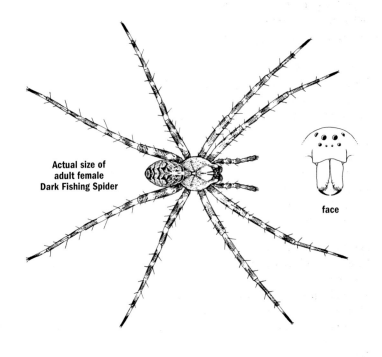

**Actual size of
adult female
Dark Fishing Spider**

face

Six-spotted Fishing Spider   *Dolomedes triton*

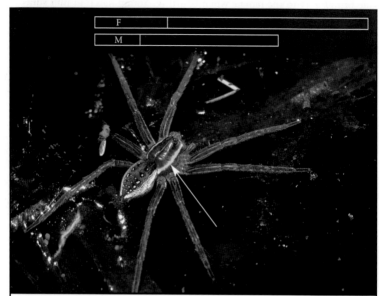

| F | |
| M | |

Around or near water; slow moving streams, ponds, lakes and swamps. Also stream banks, under rocks, docks and bridges.

Nature Notes:

Because of their long legspan, people often exaggerate the size of fishing spiders they encounter. They do not span a human hand! Even so, they are still one of the largest spiders in the North Woods.

Reported to be able to stay underwater for up to thirty minutes! Catches small fish and tadpoles along with their regular diet of aquatic insects.

Some reports of fishing spiders actually fishing. They will dip a leg in the water and wave it about hoping to attract minnows.

Description: Female's body is 17 to 20 mm long. Male's is 9 to 13 mm. Legspans range from 50 to 75 mm.

Abdomen: Two rows of six prominent light spots ↑ on a dark background. Wide light stripes run down each side.

Carapace: Dark with white to yellow stripes running down the sides ↑. An orange to white trident shape can be seen on some.

Legs: Long and thin with hairs.

Males and females are similar in color.

Hunting Technique: Usually seen motionless on floating vegetation along edges of lakes and ponds. Hunts by resting front three pair of legs on surface of water to detect ripples from potential prey. Can dive below the water to take aquatic insects and occasionally small fish.

Web: None. Only a nursery web for the young.

Fishing spiders have the ability to walk on the surface of the water. The small abdomen indicates that this is a male.

Egg Sac & Eggs: Egg sacs are produced in summer, wrapped in silk and made into a large sphere which the female carries in her jaws. She is unable to feed until the spiderlings emerge.

A Six-spotted Fishing Spider in hunting mode. The six legs on the water pick up vibrations from nearby or struggling prey.

Life Cycle:

Adults mature in spring and can be seen throughout the summer. Egg sacs are produced in summer. Spiders hibernate near water under stones, loose bark, etc. in the penultimate instar.

Dark Fishing Spider   *Dolomedes tenebrosus*

F

M

Found further from water than other fishing spiders; cabins, decks, outhouses. Often near water; slow moving streams, ponds, lakes and swamps. May climb up on docks and shoreline rocks.

Nature Notes:

Dolomedes tenebrosus is easily the largest spider regularly found in the North Woods. In North America it is only surpassed by the Carolina Wolf Spider (*Hogna carolinensis*) which has a legspan of up to four inches!

Frequently wander far from water. They are seen in cabins and outhouses and mistaken for wolf spiders.

Description: Female's body is 15 to 26 mm long. Male's is 7 to 13 mm. Legspans range from 50 to 90 mm.

Abdomen: Dark with the posterior showing several diagnostic chevron markings ↑. Light central bands bordered by black.

Carapace: Dark with pale median stripe. Black face bordered by white or tan.

Legs: Long and thin with hairs. Legs are usually annulated.

Males and females are similar in color.

Hunting Technique: Stalks prey on land and in and on buildings. Will eat prey larger than itself including adult crickets. Wanders far from water in its hunting forays.

Web: None, but a nursery web is made out of silk and folded leaves for newly emerged young.

Dolomedes tenebrosus, although a fishing spider, often wanders far from water. This one was photographed at a cabin nearly 100 yards from the nearest stream and a half mile from the nearest pond. Many cabin-dwellers see these harmless spiders in their outhouse or cabin and mistakenly call them "wolf spiders". Their faces are strikingly patterned.

Egg Sac & Eggs: Egg sacs are produced in summer, wrapped in silk and made into a large sphere which the female carries in her jaws. She is unable to feed until the spiderlings emerge.

This photo gives you a great perspective on just how big these spiders can appear when their legs are spread wide. In actuality, the largest span is only three and a half inches.

Life Cycle:

Adults mature in spring and can be seen throughout the summer. Egg sacs are produced in summer. Spiders hibernate near water, under stones or loose bark, in the penultimate instar.

Striped Fishing Spider   *Dolomedes scriptus*

Around or near water; slow moving streams, ponds, lakes and swamps. Also stream banks, under rocks, docks and bridges.

Nature Notes:

Most live near water and have been reported catching small fishes and tadpoles along with their regular diet of aquatic insects.

A nursery web is made for the newly hatched spiderlings.

Description: Female's body is 17 to 24 mm long. Male's is 13 to 16 mm. Legspans range from 55 to 80 mm.

Abdomen: The light w-shaped markings ↑ and the light stripes running down each side are diagnostic and separate this species from the darker *D. tenebrosus*.

Carapace: Dark with a very wide tan or white stripe running down each side ↑. Also a faint, forked median line.

Legs: Long and thin with hairs. Legs are usually annulated.

Males and females are similar in color.

Hunting Technique: Usually seen motionless along edges of lakes and ponds on floating vegetation. Hunts by resting front three pair of legs on surface of water to detect ripples from potential prey. Can dive below the water to take aquatic insects and occasionally small fish.

Capturing a minnow is no problem for *Dolomedes scriptus*. They regularly dive underwater to feed on aquatic insects and small fish. This species is more connected to the water than its cousin, *Dolomedes tenebrosus*.

Web: None. Nursery web is made for young.

Egg Sac & Eggs: Egg sacs are produced in summer, wrapped in silk and made into a large sphere which the female carries in her jaws. She is unable to feed until the spiderlings emerge.

Life Cycle: Adults mature in spring and can be seen throughout the summer. Egg sacs are produced in summer. Spiders hibernate near water under stones, loose bark, etc. in the penultimate instar.

The Pisauridae females all carry their precious egg sacs in this way; carried under the body and held by the jaws and attached to the spinnerets (note silk). (This is not *Dolomedes scriptus*.)

Nursery Web Spider *Pisaurina mira*

Meadows, moist open woods and edges of forests. Hunts from tall grasses, wild flowers and bushes. Not as dependent on nearby water as its relatives, the *Dolomedes* fishing spiders.

Nature Notes:

When courting, the male will present the female with a fly. If she takes it, they mate; if not, he eats it himself.

I have found several guarded nests, or nursery webs, on milkweed, though they are reported to be on poison ivy too.

On rare occasions I have collected them on the surface of the snow; usually in early winter in swamps.

Description: Female's body is 12 to 17 mm long. Male's is 10 to 15 mm. Legspans range from 35 to 45 mm.

Abdomen: About twice as long as wide. Dark brown central band that is bordered by a wavy cream-colored line ↑.

Carapace: Slightly longer than wide. Light brown with a straight cream-lined dark brown band in the center.

Eyes: Ringed with black.

Legs: Hairy, long and mostly brown. They look fuzzy.

Chelicerae: Reddish-brown.

Hunting Technique: *Pisaurina* spiders are wandering hunters on vegetation.

Web: None built for hunting, though a nursery web to hold the eggs is made by winding silk over a folded leaf. This gives the spider its common name.

This is an unusual photo of a nursery web spider carrying her egg sac. Immediately after making the sac they stash it in the nursery web and stand guard over it until the young hatch.

Egg Sac & Eggs: Egg sacs are produced in mid-summer and guarded by the female until the spiderlings hatch and disperse in late summer. Female will carry the egg sac in her jaws before making the nursery web.

Life Cycle: Adults are mature in summer. Egg sacs are produced in mid-summer. Young disperse in late summer. Overwinter as young.

A nursery web is made by wrapping green leaves with silk. It will be a safe haven for the *Pisaurina* spiderlings.

Wolf Spiders
Family Lycosidae

Lycosids may be best known as the large, hairy spiders that run across the floor or ground in the dark.

Description

Medium to large spiders (5 to 20 mm). Mostly brown, with or without stripes. Large posterior median eyes (PME). Good vision.

Abdomen: Ovoid. Brown, dark or gray and striped or spotted. Short setae hairs.

Carapace: High and longer than wide. Black, brown or gray. Some with stripes.

Eyes: Eight eyes in three rows; four in front (anterior eyes), two small posterior median eyes (PME) and two large posterior lateral eyes (PLE). Tapetum layer in eyes allows them to hunt in the dark. It also reflects light when hit by a flashlight causing the eyes to shine green.

Legs: Long and strong with many spines. Three claws.

Chelicerae: Large and powerful with teeth.

Similar Spiders

Pisaurids (nursery web spiders) are also large and brown-gray, but they have smaller eyes and are more likely near, or on, the water. Agelenids (funnel weavers) are also brown and often with stripes. But they have smaller eyes, long spinnerets and make sheet webs with funnel retreats.

Habitat

Nearly every available habitat: forest floors, grassy meadows, prairies, marshes, beaches, buildings and subterranean spaces.

Hunting Technique

Solitary active hunters by day or night. Most live on the ground and hunt at night. Capture prey by pursuing, pouncing and biting. Jaws strong enough to crush prey.

Web

No hunting snares are constructed. Some make tubular tunnel retreats while others use cracks and crevices to hide.

Observations

Spend the winter under the snow and are occasionally observed on the snow's surface. Male courts female by rhythmically waving his palps. The name "wolf spider" comes from Europe where they were once believed to hunt in packs.

Egg Sac & Eggs

The egg sac is globular; white, gray or brown. It is carried by the female and attached to her spinnerets. Hatched-young cling to special knobbed hairs (setae) on the female's abdomen. She carries them around for days.

Diversity

About 300 species are found in North America. Seven genera included in this guide.

Alopecosa	*Geolycosa*	*Hogna*	*Pirata*
Arctosa	*Gladicosa*	*Pardosa*	

Wolf Spiders (Family Lycosidae)

112 Northern Wolf Spider (*Alopecosa*)   116 Burrowing Wolf Spider (*Geolycosa*)
113 Striped Wolf Spider (*Gladicosa*)   118 Forest Wolf Spider (*Hogna*)
114 Beach Wolf Spider (*Arctosa*)   119 Thin-legged Wolf Spider (*Pardosa*)
115 Wolf Spider species (*Arctosa*)   120 Pirate Wolf Spider (*Pirata*)

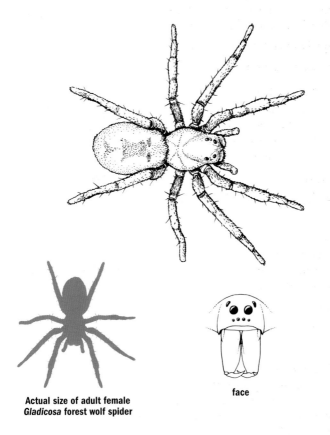

**Actual size of adult female
Gladicosa forest wolf spider**

face

Northern Wolf Spider   probably *Alopecosa aculeata*

Sunlit forest glades and shrubby meadows. Spiders roam over the forest leaf litter and ground cover. Some live in silk-lined burrows in soil or moss.

Nature Notes:

Mainly a northern genus. Some species are even found in the high arctic.

Formerly the *Alopecosa* spiders were placed in the *Lycosa* or *Tarentula* genera.

Note the large PME (posterior median eyes) that all wolf spiders possess.

Description: Female's body is 8 to 11 mm long. Male's is 7 to 10 mm. Legspans range from 15 to 22 mm.

Abdomen: Dark central mark towards the front of the abdomen; sometimes called a "heart mark". May be lance-shaped or nearly absent but will still show two dark spots anteriorly ↑. Pair of dark lateral bands; chevrons on posterior.

Carapace: A few dark lines radiating from the dorsal groove. Lateral areas are dark reddish-brown to nearly black. Gray median line is widest just behind the eyes ↑.

Legs: Reddish-brown with hairs and spines.

Chelicerae: Dark reddish-brown.

Hunting Technique: Like other Lycosids, they run after prey over the ground.

Web: None.

Egg Sac & Eggs: Eggs formed in summer. The spherical egg sac is carried by the female.

Life Cycle: Adults are found from spring through fall. Eggs formed in summer. May overwinter in a shallow silk-lined burrow.

Striped Wolf Spider sp. *Gladicosa* species

Oak forests and other woodlands. Dead leaves on the forest floor.

Description: Female's body is 11 to 14 mm long. Male's is 10 to 12 mm. Legspans range from 25 to 35 mm.

Abdomen: Gray-brown with two wide bands ↑ extending along the edge. Bands are longer on the males than the females.

Carapace: Gray-brown to orange-brown with two dark bands ↑ near the lateral edges.

Legs: Fairly long. Yellowish to orange with light rings with spines.

Hunting Technique: Like other Lycosids, they run after prey.

Web: None. Actively hunt at night, but occasionally seen during the daytime.

Egg Sac & Eggs: Eggs formed in summer. The spherical egg sac is carried by the female.

Life Cycle: Forest wolf spiders mature in the fall but courtship, mating and egg-laying wait until the following spring.

Nature Notes:

G. gulosa has been called "the drumming spider" since males rapidly vibrate their palps and abdomen while courting. Such sounds when made in fallen leaves can be heard at a distance of several feet; usually in the spring.

Gladicosa was formerly in the genus *Lycosa*.

Beach Wolf Spider *Arctosa littoralis,*

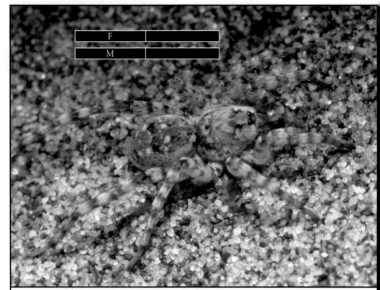

F	
M	

Sandy beaches of lakes and sandy soils. Makes burrows in sand about six to ten inches long.

Nature Notes:

I have watched these spiders on lakeshore beach sands at night by using a flashlight. This beauty was photographed on Lake Superior's Minnesota Point.

When motionless on the sand they can be nearly impossible to see. They run in short bursts and then stop and virtually disappear, so perfect is their camouflage coloration.

Its European cousin, *Arctosa perita,* is called the "sand runner."

Description: Female's body is 11 to 20 mm long. Male's is the same length. Legspans average 40 mm.

Abdomen: Yellowish-brown with brown reticulations. Spotted with flecks of gray, tan, brown, cream and white. Similar in color to the sand in the habitat where they live.

Carapace: Flattened and cryptically-colored like the abdomen. Lacks a light median stripe.

Males and females are similar.

Hunting Technique: Spiders actively hunt at night; running after their prey on sandy beaches.

Web: None.

Egg Sac & Eggs: Females produce a white egg sac. During the day she stays in a silk-lined burrow to guard the eggs.

Life Cycle: Maturity is reached in summer. Probably overwinter as immatures.

Wolf Spider sp. *Arctosa* species

F

M

Sand dunes and beaches. Shorelines of rivers and lakes.

Description: Female's body is 7 to 20 mm long. Male's is 5 to 11 mm. Legspans range from 20 to 40 mm.

Abdomen: Entire body covered with long white or gray hairs. Dark radiating pattern in middle.

Carapace: Low, wide and hairy. Evenly-colored and darker than abdomen.

Legs: Stout, evenly-colored and hairy.

Hunting Technique: Nocturnal active hunters. Wander across dunes and beaches in search of insect prey.

Web: None.

Egg Sac & Eggs: Females often create silk-lined burrows in sandy soil in which they stay with the egg sac during the day.

Life Cycle: Maturity is reached in summer. Probably overwinter as immatures.

Nature Notes:

Like *Arctosa littoralis*, this species also hunts in sandy areas. This one was photographed at night on a sandy beach of northern Lake Michigan.

Female may stay in silk-lined burrows with their eggs during the day

Nocturnal hunters. Roam the beaches and banks by night.

Burrowing Wolf Spider *Geolycosa missouriensis*

F

M

Sandy beaches and dunes. Dig burrows in sandy soil.

Nature Notes:

Burrow entrance is about ⅜-inch (1cm) in diameter. Spiders can be dug out by placing a stem of grass in the burrow. When the spider grabs the grass, they can be dug out. Once out of the burrow, they may sit without moving as if confused by the strange environment.

Only found on suitable dunes and sandy beaches in the upper Great Lakes region of the North Woods.

Description: Female's body is 18 to 22 mm long. Male's is 14 to 20 mm. Legspans range from 30 to 40 mm.

Abdomen: Wide. Sandy gray to brown with indistinct black markings.

Carapace: Similar to, but a bit darker than, the abdomen. Some light-coloring on top.

Legs: Front legs are heavy and strong.

Chelicerae: Jaws are substantial since they are used for digging.

Males may be a bit lighter than females.

Hunting Technique: Spiders live in vertical burrows up to 36-inches deep in sandy soil. Spider cements sand particles with silk for walls. Loose sand is discarded. Hunting is done at night. They hunt by lying in wait for prey at the entrance of their burrow.

Web: None.

A patient Burrowing Wolf Spider waiting for insect prey in its neatly dug sand burrow. The burrow is about ⅜ -inch across and up to 36-inches deep. The spider lines the burrow with silk which cements the sand together preventing collapse.

Egg Sac & Eggs: Egg sacs are kept underground except for warm days when the female takes them to the door.

Life Cycle: Spiders seldom emerge from burrows. They go down to escape danger. Adult males will leave the burrow during breeding season.

To see this species it is necessary to dig them out. When a piece of grass is stuck down the burrow the spider grabs on. You can now dig around the entrance and free the spider.

The eyes tell all. Wolf spiders have four small anterior median eyes (AME), two small posterior lateral eyes (PLE) and two large posterior median eyes (PME).

Forest Wolf Spider *Hogna frondicola*

F	
M	

Among leaf litter and around logs on the forest floor.

Nature Notes:

Formerly the *Hogna* spiders were placed in the *Lycosa* genus.

Spiders hunt at night and hide among the litter by day.

Notice how the dark abdomen stripes run only part way down the sides.

Description: Female's body is 11 to 14 mm long. Male's is 9 to 12 mm. Legspans range from 25 to 35 mm.

Abdomen: Gray with black stripes that only run part way down the abdomen ↑; paired central black spots ↑. A series of chevron markings may be visible on the posterior end.

Carapace: Two wide dark brown bands ↑ on sides with very narrow light submarginal stripe; lighter gray in middle.

Legs: Long and hairy. Yellowish to orange.

Hunting Technique: Unlike many wolf spiders, they hunt during the day.

Web: None. No retreat is made either.

Egg Sac & Eggs: In spring they form a spherical egg sac.

Life Cycle: Mature in late fall and overwinter as adults. Mate in spring. May live for two years.

Thin-legged Wolf Spider sp. *Pardosa* species

Open sites such as marshes, fields, bogs, quarries, beaches, rocky shores, dunes and lawns. Also leaf litter of conifer woods.

Description: Female's body is 4 to 10 mm long. Male's is 4 to 8 mm. Legspans range from 18 to 25 mm.

Abdomen: Ovoid. Many species are dark with yellow to gray irregular spots and black chevrons. May have light heart-mark and a light median band.

Carapace: Dark with a lighter–often yellow–median band on the sides.

Legs: Long and very thin ↑. Yellow, with or without rings. Hairs and spines. Long metatarsi and tarsi.

Hunting Technique: Unlike many wolf spiders, they hunt during the day.

Web: None. No retreat is made either.

Egg Sac & Eggs: Egg sacs are formed in summer. Sacs begin as a greenish sphere but become dirty-gray over time.

Life Cycle: Adults can be found all year long. Mate in spring. Egg sacs are formed in summer.

Nature Notes:

Unlike many of the wolf spiders (Lycosidae), *Pardosa* are small and active in the sunlight.

Due to their long legs, they carry their bodies quite high.

A very large genus with more than one hundred species.

A female thin-legged wolf spider carries the egg sac with her. Note the very thin legs that distinguish members of the *Pardosa*.

Family *Lycosidae* WOLF SPIDERS

Pirate Wolf Spider   *Pirata piraticus*

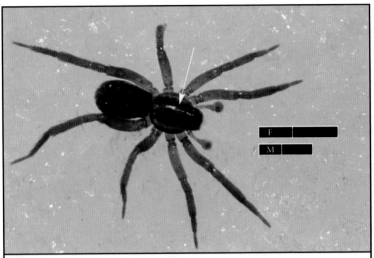

F

M

Marshes, swamps, bogs, streams, lakes and shorelines of ponds.

Nature Notes:

One of the smallest of our wolf spiders.

Often collected in wet areas next to water. Spiders can and will walk on the surface of water.

Pirate Wolf Spiders are able to duck under water to prey on mosquito larvae.

Penultimate spiders often seen and collected on the surface of the snow all winter.

Description: Female's body is 6 to 9 mm long. Male's is 5 to 6 mm. Legspans range from 15 to 22 mm.

Abdomen: Light longitudinal stripe on anterior half; indistinct chevron behind. Paired yellow spots on posterior half. May be reddish-brown in center. Many light hairs.

Carapace: High. Light yellow band on each side. Three pale bands run from eyes posterior uniting to form one band. Dark Y-shaped mark in middle ↑. (May look like a tuning fork.)

Legs: Yellow-brown to green.

Hunting Technique: Hunts on the ground by day and night.

Web: None to catch prey. Some may build silken tubes from sphagnum to water. Females make temporary retreats under stones.

Egg Sac & Eggs: Egg sacs are produced in summer until early fall.

Life Cycle: Adults can be found in summer. Egg sacs are produced in summer. Winter is spent as penultimates or other young instars.

Funnel Weavers
Family Agelenidae

Agelenids are best known as the makers of funnel webs so often seen in yards, parks and along roadsides in late summer. Only common brown spider with long spinnerets in our area.

Description

Medium-sized spiders (10 to 20 mm). Body is brown with markings. Long spinnerets are visible from above.

Abdomen: Oval and elongated. Brown, gray or dark; usually with patterns of dots or bars.

Carapace: Rather flat but broadly rounded and sloping from the head. Often brown with light stripes.

Eyes: Two strongly curved rows of equally-sized eyes.

Legs: Brown, long and hairy with three claws.

Spinnerets: Long posterior spinnerets that are easily seen from above.

Chelicerae: Jaws with three teeth.

Similar Spiders

Hahniids have a similar web (no funnel) and are much smaller. Lycosids (wolf spiders) may look the same, but they do not have long spinnerets, make no webs and have large posterior median eyes (PME).

Habitat

Common in areas of rock, grass or on walls; anywhere the funnel web can be built to provide a hidden retreat. Funnel weavers can also live in, and on, buildings; including basements, window sills and porches.

Hunting Technique

These spiders hunt by sitting in the entrance of the funnel-shaped retreat, feeling for the vibrations of struggling prey. They rapidly run out to retrieve any victims and bring them back to the funnel to eat.

Web

Hunting snares are usually sheet webs spread out over the grass with a built-in tubular funnel retreat. Such webs can be abundant on grass in late summer. Silk is non-sticky. Smaller spiders may make a web without a retreat.

Observations

Spiders may overwinter indoors. Occasionally seen in colder times of the year in sinks and bath tubs; these are adults seeking water who get trapped by the slippery porcelain sides.

Egg Sac & Eggs

Egg sacs are disc-shaped and deposited in crevices and cracks near the web in fall.

Diversity

About 300 species are found in North America. Two genera in this guide.

Agelenopsis
Tegenaria

Funnel Weavers (Family Agelenidae)

124 Grass Spider species *(Agelenopsis)*
126 Barn Funnel Weaver *(Tegenaria)*

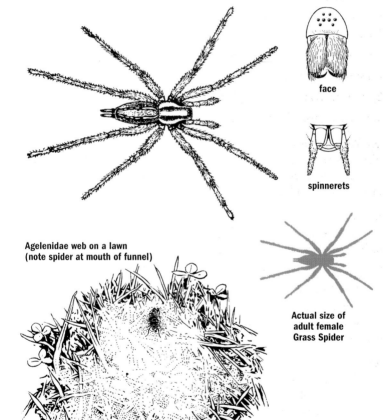

face

spinnerets

**Agelenidae web on a lawn
(note spider at mouth of funnel)**

**Actual size of
adult female
Grass Spider**

Grass Spider sp. *Agelenopsis* species

Grassy areas, low shrubs, stone piles and corners of buildings: both inside and out.

Nature Notes:

Webs may be abundant on lawns and in grasses during late summer.

I have found hundreds of tiny webs, less than two inches in diameter, on July days. Two months later, in the same yards, the webs will be over six inches in diameter.

Spiders that live on or in buildings may survive far into the fall and the webs may last years.

Due to their color patterns, these spiders can be confused with wolf spiders, but their long spinnerets are diagnostic.

Description: Female's body is 10 to 17 mm long. Male's is 9 to 15 mm. Legspans range from 25 to 35 mm.

Abdomen: Brown or gray; may have a light stripe down the middle. Darker bands towards the sides with gray at the edge. Spinnerets extend well beyond the end of the abdomen.

Carapace: Three pale stripes and two dark stripes ↑.

Legs: Long and thin.

Spinnerets: As characteristic of this family, they have long lateral spinnerets that can be seen from above ↑. This is not true for most spider families.

Hunting Technique: Grass spiders will usually hunt by sitting in the entrance of the funnel-shaped retreat, feeling for web vibrations. They rapidly run out to retrieve any victims and bring them back to the funnel retreat to eat.

Note the funnel-shaped retreat near the top of the web. When an insect falls onto the sheet web the spider runs out of the funnel to grab it.

On foggy mornings in late summer the webs of the funnel weavers stand out. Dozens may be scattered over a single lawn. Without condensed water droplets coating the webs, they are nearly invisible.

Web: Horizontal sheet web with a funnel near one edge. Threads are not sticky. Webs made in low grass of lawns, taller grasses, shrubs and basements. Dewy mornings reveal the presence of these hunting snares.

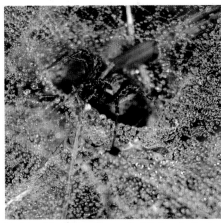

Egg Sac & Eggs: Eggs overwinter in sacs that are hidden near the web.

Life Cycle: Dispersal occurs in spring. Young build small webs in early summer; large ones in late summer. Eggs overwinter.

A grass spider waits at the mouth of its funnel retreat for victims. The threads are not sticky so the spider must be ready to rush out at the slightest web vibration.

Family *Agelenidae* FUNNEL WEAVERS

Barn Funnel Weaver *Tegenaria domestica*

F

M

Frequently in homes, barns and basements; anywhere it is dark. Outdoors they may live under stones and in rock crevices. Also found in quarries and woodlands.

Nature Notes:

Barn Funnel Weavers may live for three to four years.

After a single mating, the female may produce up to nine sets of eggs over two years.

During the breeding season, the female and male can live peaceably in the same web.

Description: Female's body is 7 to 12 mm long. Male's is 6 to 9 mm. Legspans range from 20 to 30 mm.

Abdomen: Dark gray with irregular spots on a light background. Three dark spots in a line posteriorly.

Carapace: Yellowish with two gray bands.

Legs: Long and faintly ringed.

Chelicerae: Slightly convex with four to six teeth.

Hunting Technique: Sit and wait in the funnel retreat that is built into the web.

Web: Funnel webs are built in dark moist rooms or cellars; often in corners. Funnel leads to the retreat. Irregular snare lines in a concave pattern above the sheet.

Egg Sac & Eggs: Egg sac formed in summer. Placed on the snare lines of the web and covered with soil and wood chips.

Life Cycle: Adults may be found all year long. Mating and formation of egg sacs in summer. During maturation, spiders molt nine times.

There is an explanation for why these two photographs were taken indoors; Barn Funnel Weavers are very common in houses.

Hahnid Spiders
Family Hahniidae

Hahniids are tiny spiders that are seldom seen. We may only notice their small sheet webs when dew-covered.

Description

Very small spiders (1 to 3 mm). Brown, with all six spinnerets arranged in a single transverse row.

Abdomen: Ovoid. Brown, with patterns. Abdomen is larger than the carapace.

Carapace: Ovoid and brown.

Eyes: Arranged in two recurved rows.

Legs: Nearly equal in length and spined. Three claws.

Spinnerets: All six are arranged in a single transverse row. The outer ones are the largest.

Similar Spiders

No other spiders show this spinneret arrangement, but Micryphantids (dwarf spiders) are just as small and also make small sheet webs.

Habitat

On, or in, soils of forests, meadows, fields, gardens and lawns. More likely in damp places. Often among soil particles or mosses.

Hunting Technique

Spiders usually remain at the edge of their tiny webs.

Web

Small sheet webs, usually less than two inches in diameter. The delicate webs are common in moss and slight depressions such as footprints or animal tracks. Usually invisible unless dew-covered. No funnel retreat is constructed.

Egg Sac & Eggs

Egg sac is circular and covered with white silk.

Diversity
About 20 species are found in North America. One genus in this guide.

Neoantistea

Hahnid Spiders (Family Hahniidae)
130 Hahnid Spider species (*Neoantistea*)

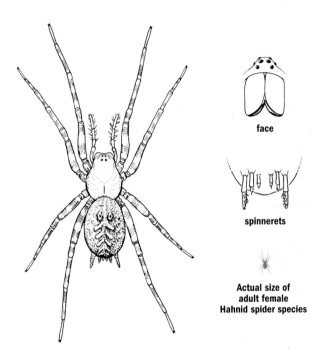

face

spinnerets

**Actual size of
adult female
Hahnid spider species**

Hahnid Spider sp. *Neoantistea* species

Forests, meadows and fields. Among clumps of soil at the edge of their webs. Take refuge in crevices of soil, moss or under the leaf litter.

Nature Notes:

The web pictured above is only the diameter of a fifty-cent piece! Tiny spiders usually make tiny webs.

These miniscule spiders are hard to see, but look for them on the edge of a tiny sheet web that is only a couple of inches across.

When magnified, the row of six spinnerets become visible, making the spider easy to identify as a member of the Hahniidae.

Description: Female's body is 2.5 to 3.5 mm long. Male's is 2 to 3 mm. Legspan ranges from 5 to 6 mm.

Carapace: Nearly as broad as long. Reddish to orange-brown.

Abdomen: Gray with a pattern of yellow spots.

Legs: Yellowish and ringed with gray.

Spinnerets: Spread to form a lateral transverse row. All six are visible from above.

Hunting Technique: Sit and wait for prey next to their tiny web.

Web: Small, delicate sheet web that is only a couple inches across. No retreat is used. Placed close to the ground and often near water, moist soil or moss. Rarely in dry places or under stones. May be found in depressions formed by animal tracks. Webs are difficult to see unless they are covered with dew. Spiders stay at the edge of the web.

Egg Sac & Eggs: Egg sacs are circular and covered with silk.

Life Cycle: Mature in the fall and winter.

Lynx Spiders
Family Oxyopidae

Oxyopids are best known by their long spiny legs and their active daytime hunting.

Description

Medium-sized spiders (5 to 10 mm) with many spines on their long legs.

Abdomen: Broad in front, tapering to the posterior tip. Often with striped patterns.

Carapace: Yellowish with striped pattern. Longer than wide. The face is vertical.

Eyes: Eight eyes; six larger eyes forming a hexagon and two small anterior eyes. This arrangement makes them appear to be a six-eyed spider. As expected in an active-hunting spider, they have very good vision.

Legs: Light-colored with some dark bands. Legs long with many spines projecting at angles. Three claws.

Similar Spiders

Though Oxyopids do not look like Salticids (jumping spiders), they actively hunt in the daytime and so have similar habits. Salticids have shorter legs and larger eyes.

Habitat

Meadows, fields, yards, tall grasses and shrubs.

Hunting Technique

Using good vision and long legs, they actively pursue prey over plants in the daytime. They will also lay in ambush for potential prey. As hunters they may superficially resemble the Salticids (jumping spiders) or the Lycosids (wolf spiders), but they have been described as hunting like two other animals; like a lynx, they stalk and pounce; like a mantis, they sit and wait.

Web

No hunting snares or retreats are constructed.

Egg Sac & Eggs

Egg sac is anchored by a dragline in vegetation and guarded by the female.

Diversity

About 20 species are found in North America. One genus in this guide.

Oxyopes

Lynx Spiders (Family Oxyopidae)

134 Striped Lynx Spider (*Oxyopes)*

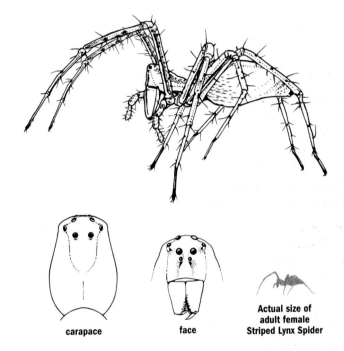

carapace

face

**Actual size of
adult female
Striped Lynx Spider**

Striped Lynx Spider   *Oxyopes salticus*

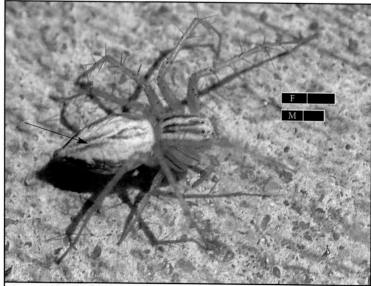

Hunt in the daytime in a variety of habitats. Most common on low vegetation, herbaceous plants and occasionally in trees.

Nature Notes:

Status of Striped Lynx Spiders in the North Woods is uncertain. Its close cousin, *Oxyopes scalaris*, the Western Lynx Spider is more common in the North.

Like a lynx, they hunt by stalking and pouncing.

Usually seen actively hunting or ambushing prey during summer days.

Good eyesight.

Description: Female's body is 6 to 7 mm long. Male's is 5 to 6 mm. Legspans range from 12 to 15 mm.

Abdomen: Attractively patterned. Lighter than carapace on top ↑, darker on sides. Male is darker with iridescent scales. In the Western Lynx Spider (*O. scalaris*) the abdomen is darker than the carapace.

Carapace: Mostly yellow with four longitudinal gray bands. A pair of black lines extend from the AME down onto the chelicerae ↑. Western Lynx Spider (*O. scalaris*) has no distinct black lines on the face.

Legs: Yellow with many spines ↑.

Hunting Technique: Striped Lynx Spiders are daylight hunters; sometimes actively pursuing prey and other times waiting in ambush.

Web: None.

Striped Lynx Spiders certainly are distinctive. Note the spiny legs, high carapace and black lines on the face.

Egg Sac & Eggs: Egg sac is formed in summer and guarded by the female.

Life Cycle: Adults may be found all summer. Egg sacs are formed in summer. Appear to overwinter as immatures.

Ground Spiders (Running Spiders) Family Gnaphosidae

If we see gnaphosids at all, we usually see them scampering quickly across the ground.

Description

Medium-sized spiders (10 to 15 mm). Often uniformly-colored, but some with spots and patterns.

Abdomen: Elongated and slightly flattened. Usually dark, but some spots, lines or patterns.

Carapace: Ovoid. Usually dark brown or red with no spots or markings

Eyes: Two transverse rows; anterior median eyes (AME) are dark while the posterior median eyes (PME) are oval and at an angle.

Legs: Medium in length. All legs nearly equal in length and stout with spines. Two claws.

Spinnerets: Front and side spinnerets are cylindrical and separated. They are visible from above.

Similar Spiders

Clubionids (sac spiders) are similar in shape, but are usually lighter in color. Eyes are in a different pattern and not oval. Spinnerets of sac spiders are not cylindrical.

Habitat

On or near the ground in grasslands, leaf litter, under stones and cracks in tree trunks.

Hunting Technique

Active hunters that usually pursue prey on the ground. Fast runners that hunt at night. During the day they hide in retreats or under stones or bark.

Web

No hunting snares are formed, but tubular retreats are made under rocks and in rolled leaves. Male may construct a retreat next to a female.

Observations

Mature in late spring to early summer. Adults can be found all year long. Males pursue females along her dragline.

Egg Sac & Eggs

Egg sac is a shiny pink or white papery disc attached to the underside of stones or placed in retreats. The egg sacs are produced in late summer.

Diversity
About 300 species are found in North America. Two genera in this guide.

> *Gnaphosa*
> *Herpyllus*

Ground Spiders (Family Gnaphosidae)
138 Ground Spider species (*Gnaphosa*)
139 Parson Spider (*Herpyllus*)

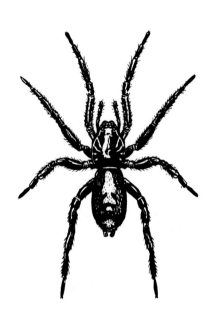

face

spinnerets

**Actual size of
adult female
Parson Spider**

Ground Spider sp. probably *Gnaphosa muscorum*

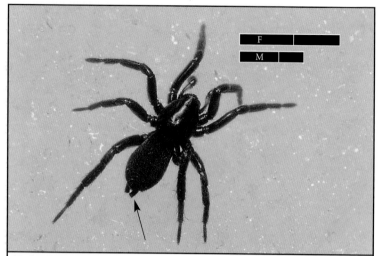

Under stones and fallen logs in woods. On the ground in pastures. May be under mosses or bark in pine and spruce forests.

Description: Female's body is 9 to 15 mm long. Male's is 7 to 12 mm. Legspans range from 18 to 28 mm.

Abdomen: Dark gray to black and covered with fine hairs that are longer and coarser toward the rear.

Carapace: Nearly as long as the abdomen. Dark brown with black markings along the radial furrows.

Legs: Thick and strong. Evenly brown with hair.

Spinnerets: Dark, cylindrical ↑ and visible from above.

Hunting Technique: Nocturnal hunters who use their running ability to chase down prey.

Web: None. But they may make silken retreats under stones in which to hide during the day.

Egg Sac & Eggs: Egg sac is produced in summer. Female stands guard over this flattened sac which is not attached to any object.

Life Cycle: Adults mature in spring and summer. Egg sac is produced in summer. They appear to overwinter as both adults and young.

Nature Notes:

I have collected young and adults on the snow's surface in early winter (see photo above).

Males wander more than females.

Usually, we see these spiders as they quickly run over the ground.

Parson Spider *Herpyllus ecclesiastica*

Under stones, boards or on the ground in wooded areas. Also found in buildings.

Description: Female's body is 9 to 13 mm long. Male's is 5 to 6 mm. Legspans range from 12 to 25 mm.

Abdomen: Longer than the carapace. Gray to black; whitish band in the center ↑ (front two-thirds) with light spots behind. Males have a conspicuous brown abdominal scutum. Body is covered with silky gray hairs.

Carapace: Longer than wide. Chestnut-brown with whitish central stripe.

Legs: Similar in color to the carapace.

Spinnerets: Long and cylindrical. They can be seen from above.

Hunting Technique: Pursue prey at night.

Web: None.

Egg Sac & Eggs: Egg sac is produced during the summer and guarded by the female.

Life Cycle: Adults can be found nearly any time of the year. Egg sac is produced in the summer. Overwinter as an adult or as young in a silken cocoon placed under bark.

Nature Notes:

Called the Parson Spider because of its black and white vestments.

A spider of the forest floor that is usually seen scurrying about.

A very fast moving spider. It may be our fastest North Woods species.

Sac Spiders
Family Clubionidae

Clubionids are best known by the white resting sacs they construct in rolled leaves or other hiding places. Some clubionids are now placed in the family Miturgidae. Several species mimic ants.

Description

Small to medium spiders (3 to 15 mm). Usually light in color.

Abdomen: Ovoid and elongated; rounded dorsally. Often light in color. Many with medial stripes, spots or markings. Males and females are about the same size.

Carapace: Oval. Can be dark or light-colored.

Eyes: Two rows of pearly eyes. Anterior median eyes (AME) are slightly darker.

Legs: Nearly equal in length. Long, uniformly-colored and spined. Two claws.

Chelicerae: Toothed.

Spinnerets: Compact and cone-shaped. One pair visible from above.

Similar Spiders

Gnaphosids (ground spiders) are slightly bigger, darker and faster runners. They have oval posterior median eyes (PME). Spinnerets of gnaphosids are cylindrical and widely-spaced.

Habitat

On or near the ground. Low foliage.

Hunting Technique

Active hunter at night. They hide in retreats or nests during the day.

Web

No hunting snares are built. Resting nests are constructed in rolled leaves or under bark. It is these white nests that are often seen. Tubular retreats are also made in the same type of locations.

Egg Sac & Eggs

Egg sacs are produced and hidden under stones, bark or leaves.

Diversity

About 200 species are found in North America. Two genera in this guide.

Castianeira
Clubiona

Sac Spiders (Family Clubionidae)

142 Red-spotted Antmimic (*Castianeira*)
143 Sac Spider species (*Clubiona*)

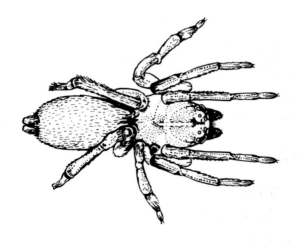

face

spinnerets

Actual size of
adult female
Sac Spider species

Red-spotted Antmimic *Castianeira descripta*

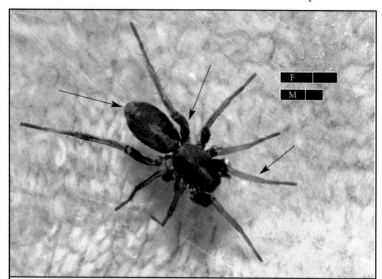

On the ground, under stones, logs and in the leaf litter. Occasionally in buildings.

Nature Notes:

The genus *Castianeira* are known as ant mimics. The closely related *C. cingulata* (Two-banded Antmimic) has been seen running in the company of carpenter ants at night and mimicing their movements. They slowly raise and wave their front legs; the motion may resemble that of the ant's antennae.

Run very rapidly when disturbed.

Description: Female's body is 8 to 9 mm long. Male's is 6 to 7.5 mm. Legspans range from 12 to 16 mm.

Abdomen: Black to dark mahogany with bright red spots ↑ at posterior end; more extensive in males. Red marks occasionally found all the way to anterior end.

Carapace: Black to dark mahogany.

Legs: Femur black ↑; outer leg segments a bit lighter ↑, especially on legs I and II.

Hunting Technique: Active hunter at night. They sometimes run with groups of carpenter ants, whom they mimic.

Web: No hunting snare is built.

Egg Sac & Eggs: During late summer, an egg sac is formed beneath stones. Very flat and disc-shaped. It is attached to the stone or other debris by sticky saliva.

Life Cycle: Adults in late summer. Egg sacs made in late summer.

Sac Spider sp. *Clubiona* species

Tall grasses near marshes, lakes and sometimes forests.

Description: Female's body is 5 to 9 mm long. Male's is 4 to 7 mm. Legspans range from 12 to 18 mm.

Abdomen: Not flattened. Often reddish-brown to brown and unmarked. *C. riparia* has a pair of yellow lines that envelope a central dark stripe that is broken into spots posteriorly.

Carapace: Light-colored and unmarked.

Legs: Fairly long with long tarsal claws and large hair tufts.

Spinnerets: Compact and cone-shaped ↑. Visible from above.

Hunting Technique: Active hunter at night.

Web: None, though they do build tubular silken retreats.

Egg Sac & Eggs: Made in early summer. Sometimes they will fold a blade of grass into a three-sided chamber to hold the egg sac. This shelter will become a nursery for the spiderlings.

Life Cycle: Adults in spring and early summer. Egg sac is made in early summer. Winter is spent under bark and stones in the penultimate stage.

Nature Notes:

This family is known for its nursery sacs. They are said to be a nursery for the spiderlings and a home for the female until she dies.

I have seen nearly mature sac spiders on the snow's surface on fairly mild winter days (see photo above).

Crab Spiders
Family Thomisidae

Thomisids are probably best known as the spiders found sitting on the blossoms of daisies, black-eyed susans or goldenrods on summer days. Some species, by changing their own body color from white to yellow or yellow to white, can match the color of the flower they hunt from. In this way they are able to blend in to their background and ambush pollinating insects. The two large front pairs of legs grab and hold prey.

Description

Medium-sized spiders (5 to 10 mm). Their bodies are wider than long with legs held in a crab-like position. Though most are drab, some are quite striking and can change their body color. Females are much larger than males.

Abdomen: Broadly oval and flat; widest near the posterior. May be patterned and quite colorful; yellow, orange, white, brown and pink are common colors.

Carapace: Flat and about as long as wide.

Eyes: Two rows of curved eyes; lateral eyes larger and on tubercles. They have good vision.

Legs: Held out and forward; crab-like. Pairs one and two are longer than pairs three and four. Two claws. With legs held out sideways, crab spiders are able to walk forward, backward and sideways.

Chelicerae: Small with no teeth.

Similar Spiders

Philodromids (running crab spiders) may appear to be the same shape, but they tend to be flatter and more gray. They also move faster and are more likely to climb trees or walls.

Habitat

Found in fields, meadows, woodlots and gardens. Frequently seen sitting on the petals of a blooming flower. Others may be found in the forest leaf litter.

Hunting Technique

Crab spiders are sedentary hunters and may sit in ambush, often in flowers, for hours. Using good eyesight and legs held ready in a grasping position, they can quickly immobilize and feed on insects bigger than themselves. Some species can change color to blend in with the vegetation, thereby camouflaging themselves from potential prey.

Web
No hunting snares, retreats, molting or hibernating webs are built. Females will fold a leaf over and tie it together with silk creating shelter for the egg sac.

Observations
Males are tiny compared to the females. Because of this, the males of some species must first tie up the huge female with silk before attempting to mate. Afterward, she is easily able to break free of her silk wraps.

Egg Sac & Eggs
Egg sacs are flat and attached to a nearby substrate. Females guard their egg sac until they die, which is often before the young even hatch.

Diversity
About 130 species are found in North America. Three genera in this guide.

> *Misumena*
> *Misumenops*
> *Xysticus*

Crab Spiders (Family Thomisidae)
146 Goldenrod Crab Spider (*Misumena*)
148 Northern Crab Spider (*Misumenops*)
150 Transverse-banded Crab Spider (*Xysticus*)

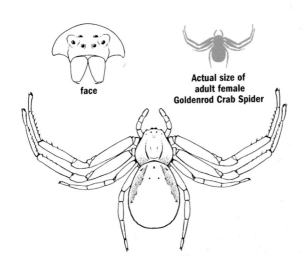

face

Actual size of
adult female
Goldenrod Crab Spider

Goldenrod Crab Spider *Misumena vatia* (female)

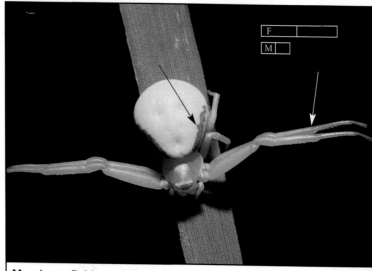

Meadows, fields and gardens. Often on goldenrods and daisies.

Nature Notes:

I have found that nearly every patch of daisies has one or two resident Goldenrod Crab Spiders during June.

Females and males look very different and it is easy to think that they represent different species. He is tiny! (See photo on page 21.)

Courting and mating take place on the same flowers that the females hunt from.

Spiders grab prey with the front legs, but continue to hold and feed on the insect without use of the legs.

Description: Female's body is 8 to 10 mm long. Male's is 3 to 4 mm. Legspans range from 8 to 20 mm.

Abdomen: White or yellow with pink-red wavy bands ↑ running down each side. Can change color from white to yellow to light green. Such a change takes several days. Male's abdomen is pale with dark edges and two median lines.

Carapace: Female's carapace is colored the same as the abdomen; usually white. Eye region may be tinged with red. Male's carapace is dark reddish-brown to red with a light spot in middle extending from the eyes.

Legs: Same color as the body. Pairs one and two are the longest and held out crab-like ↑.

Hunting Technique: Hunts during daylight hours by ambushing prey. Able to camouflage itself by changing from white to yellow to pale green to match the flower it is hunting on. Prefers to hunt from yellow and white flowers;

Goldenrod Crab Spider and honey bee in a life and death struggle on an Ox-eye Daisy. The spider has remained white to blend in with the white petals.

ox-eye daisy and black-eyed susans in early summer, goldenrods later. Grabs prey with long front legs, but once captured it only holds on with the jaws (see photo above).

Web: None.

Egg Sac & Eggs: Eggs sacs are attached to leaves.

Life cycle: Mature in early summer after which, mating takes place. Adults can be seen most of the summer. Overwinter as immatures.

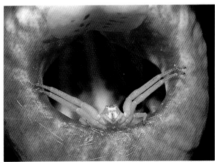

A crab spider waits for a victim at the entrance of a Showy Ladyslipper orchid. She cannot turn pink.

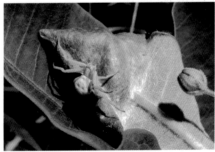

A female Goldenrod Crab Spider attaches her egg sac to a folded leaf; in this case, on a milkweed plant.

Family *Thomisidae* CRAB SPIDERS

Northern Crab Spider *Misumenops asperatus*

F
M

On flowers, grasses and other foliage. Summer meadows, road-sides, old fields and gardens.

Description: Female's body is 4 to 6 mm long. Male's is 3 to 4 mm. Legspans range from 6 to 12 mm.

Abdomen: Rounded and flat. Patterns of pink streaks and spots on the pale, often yellowish, abdomen. On posterior half, two rows of reddish spots converge toward the rear. Another pair of reddish spots are on the back towards the side ↑. Northern Crab Spiders can change color from white to yellow to pale green.

Carapace: About equal in length and width. Brownish to pale green with two pink stripes.

Eyes: On tubercles.

Legs: Pairs one and two are very long and held out crab-like. Laterigrade legs are dull yellow to off white. Pink bands on tibiae and tarsi.

Nature Notes:

Sometimes caught, paralyzed and carried off by mud dauber wasps who place the spiders in their mud tube nests. The wasps lay an egg on the spider which becomes food for the developing wasp larvae.

Not as noticeable as its cousin, the Goldenrod Crab Spider, but still common on the showy flowers of June.

This Northern Crab Spider has turned pale green to blend in more closely with the petals of the Wild Iris. Better camouflage means more meals.

Hunting Technique: Sedentary hunters in flowers. They wait and pounce.

Web: None.

Egg Sac & Eggs: Formed in summer.

Life Cycle: Mature specimens have been observed from spring to fall.

Transverse-banded Crab Spider *Xysticus transversatus*

Under bark, leaves or stones on the ground. Low plants in woods. Some may also be found in fields and meadows on flowers and grasses. Even found in bogs.

Nature Notes:

Formerly known as *Xysticus ferox.*

There are many species in this genus. Most are shades of brown or gray with white or yellow markings.

May be found on flowers, but not as likely as the white and yellow crab spiders (*Misumena* and *Misumenops* genera).

Description: Female's body is 4 to 9 mm long. Male's is 3 to 7 mm. Legspans range from 12 to 18 mm.

Abdomen: Brown with pale band around outside edges ↑. Several short black bands ↑ on posterior. Narrow light cross-bands on rear end.

Carapace: Slightly longer than wide. Yellowish with two dark brown lateral bands. Wide central light band.

Legs: Fairly long and stout. Pairs one and two are longest.

Hunting Technique: Spiders hunt in the typical crab spider manner; they wait for prey and ambush insects, grabbing them with their front legs. Eyesight is good.

Web: None.

The fingernail and goldenrod flower-head give you a good size scale to compare to this Transverse-banded Crab Spider. Like most crab spiders, these guys are slow and so must ambush prey (mainly pollinating insects) on flower heads.

Egg Sac & Eggs:

Female guards egg sac but dies before the spiderlings emerge in summer.

Life Cycle: Mature in spring with adults found all summer. Winter is spent in penultimate or younger stages.

Surprisingly, many spiders can be found on the snow on mild winter days. Here a young male *Xysticus* crab spider is out for a stroll. The "boxing gloves" on the palps tell us that this is a male.

Family *Thomisidae* CRAB SPIDERS | **151**

Running Crab Spiders
Family Philodromidae

Philodromids are best known as the fast-moving crab-spider look-alikes that run over the ground and climb tree trunks and walls. Most are mottled shades of gray.

Description

Medium-sized spiders (6 to 10 mm). Flattened slim bodies that are usually gray or brown.

Abdomen: Flat and rather elongate. Widest behind the middle. Posterior end is pointed.

Carapace: Nearly round and slightly longer than wide. Head slightly angled up. Yellow, brown or gray with lateral bands.

Eyes: Two rows of small equally-sized eyes. No tubercles. In some species the posterior median eyes (PME) combine with the anterior eyes to form a hexagon.

Legs: Nearly all the same length and thickness; often laterigrade. In *Philodromus* species, pairs one and two are longest. Two claws.

Chelicerae: Small with no teeth.

Similar Spiders

Thomisids (crab spiders) are often similarly shaped, but they are more colorful and have lateral eyes on tubercles. Crab spiders are much less likely to climb walls and trees than Philodromids.

Habitat

Ground-dweller, but also grasses, low plants and tree trunks. Perhaps the most arboreal of our spiders; often on the bark of standing trees. More abundant in the North. On mild winter days they can sometimes be seen on the snow.

Hunting Technique

With drab camouflaging coloration, they hunt both actively (running after prey) and passively (ambushing prey). They are able to move fast.

Web

No hunting snares, retreats or nests are built.

Observations

Most overwinter in subadult stage, perhaps explaining why they have been observed on the snow's surface on mild winter days.

Egg Sac & Eggs
Egg sacs are attached to bark or leaves in early summer.

Diversity
About 100 species are found in North America. Three genera in this guide.

Philodromus
Thanatus
Tibellus

Running Crab Spiders (Family Philodromidae)

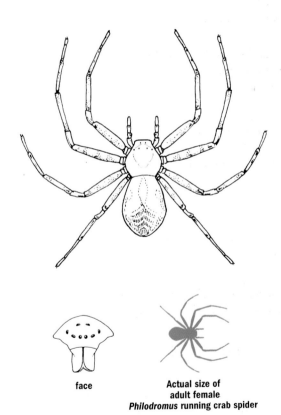

face

Actual size of
adult female
Philodromus running crab spider

Inconspicuous Running Crab Spider *Philodromus* sp.

On ground among the leaf litter. Woods; deciduous or coniferous. On tree bark and adjacent foliage. Dirt roads too.

Nature Notes:

Philodromus may be one of the most arboreal of all of our spiders. Often found hunting in and on trees.

Frequently observed indoors where they climb on walls and ceilings.

I have collected several penultimates on the surface of the snow in early winter.

When sitting still, they blend in with bark or rocks. Difficult to see when not moving. But when they move, they are fast!

Description: Female's body is 4 to 8 mm long. Male's is 4 to 6 mm. Legspans range from 15 to 20 mm.

Abdomen: Flat, longer than wide, angular at the sides and with a pointed end. Gray-brown with spots and chevrons.

Carapace: Flat, smoothly convex and as long as wide. Gray-brown with spots; a very protective coloration.

Eyes: Anterior eyes are uniform in size.

Legs: Long and thin. Laterigrade; second pair is just barely the longest ↑. Yellow-brown and striped.

Hunting Technique: Running crab spiders are active hunters. They run rapidly as they climb tree trunks, plants or the walls and ceilings of houses while in search of prey.

Web: None.

Running crab spiders are as quick as their name implies. A flattened abdomen and carapace allows them to hide under bark or rocks.

Egg Sac & Eggs: Egg sac is formed in the summer among the leaves and bark. It is guarded by the female.

Life Cycle: Spiders mature in spring and adults can be found throughout the summer and into the fall. Egg sac is formed in the summer. Winter is spent as a penultimate instar.

Penultimate instars (immature adults) can be occasionally found on top of the snow.

Diamond Spider   *Thanatus formicinus*

Grasses, bushes, branches and tree trunks. Also found on the ground.

Nature Notes:

Because of their gray-brown bodies and fairly long legs, *Thanatus* spiders can be mistaken for wolf spiders (family Lycosidae).

Named for the very distinct dark diamond shape on its abdomen.

Description: Female's body is 6 to 8 mm long. Male's is 5 to 6 mm. Legspans range from 20 to 30 mm.

Abdomen: Usually longer than the carapace. Gray-brown with a distinctive dark lance-shaped or "diamond" mark ↑ on the anterior part of the abdomen.

Carapace: Almost as wide as long. Gray-brown with a lighter pattern in the center.

Legs: Longer than most members of this family. Nearly all the legs are the same length but the second and fourth pairs are slightly longer.

Hunting Technique: Pursue prey.

Web: None.

Egg Sac & Eggs: Egg sac is cream-colored and shaped like a biconvex lens. It is attached to a leaf.

Life Cycle: Winter as adult or penultimate instar. Mature males in spring. Mature females found in spring and summer; possibly in winter.

Oblong Running Crab Spider *Tibellus oblongus*

F

M

Tall grasses and bushes. Common in meadows, fields and marshes.

Description: Female's body is 7 to 10 mm long. Male's is 6 to 8 mm. Legspans range from 18 to 25 mm.

Abdomen: Three times as long as wide. Brown median stripe on yellowish background. Near the caudal end there are two black spots ↑.

Carapace: Light yellow-gray with a brown midstripe.

Eyes: Posterior row of eyes are strongly recurved.

Legs: Long, slender and lacking dark rings. The fourth pair is the longest.

Hunting Technique: Ambush prey.

Web: None.

Egg Sac & Eggs: Eggs hatch in late summer.

Life Cycle: Both sexes mature in spring. Adults can be found all summer long. Mating takes place in summer and the egg sac hatches in late summer. They overwinter as young.

Nature Notes:

Unlike other members of this family, *Tibellus* have elongated, thin bodies. When at rest on a grass stem, they are difficult to detect due to the stripes on the body and legs held straight out front and behind.

I have collected hundreds of these spiders by using sweep nets in late summer and fall. Hard to see among the grasses, but easy to see when they are on a different substrate.

I have seen a few adults on the surface of the snow early in the season.

Jumping Spiders
Family Salticidae

Salticids, otherwise known as jumping spiders or jumpers, have big anterior median eyes (AME), short legs and hunt in the daytime. Probably best known as the lively spiders that hop around us as we sit in the sunshine.

Description

Small to medium spiders (3 to 15 mm). Male and female about equal in size.

Abdomen: Widest in the middle; tapered to posterior end. Often patterned and colorful. Sometimes with iridescent scales.

Carapace: Longer than wide and not flat. Vertical face that may be colorful and iridescent, but not as colorful as the abdomen.

Eyes: Huge anterior median eyes (AME). Great eyesight that may be the best of any invertebrate. They can recognize prey from at least twelve inches away. Able to move the anterior median eyes. The posterior lateral eyes (PLE) are far back on the head. Eyes appear to be in three rows.

Legs: Short and hairy. First pair is thickest; back legs used for jumping. Two claws.

Chelicerae: Small.

Similar Spiders

No other spiders look or act like the jumping spiders. However, some jumpers mimic ants; look for their eight legs and lack of antennae.

Habitat

Nearly always seen in sunny places; leaves, bark and walls of buildings.

Hunting Technique

Jumpers hunt in the daytime. They use their AME to locate and identify prey. They run toward it and then slow down and stalk to within striking distance. A sudden rush of blood to either the rear or third pair of legs allows them to leap several times their body length. Jumpers are not afraid to attack quarry that is larger than themselves. A silk dragline is attached to a substrate before leaping just in case they miss and need to haul themselves back up to a safe perch.

Web

No hunting snare is constructed. Closely woven retreats are made for molting, hibernating and resting. These retreats may be under bark, between stones or rolled in leaves.

Observations

Jumping spiders like the sunlight and are found in warm, sunny places. Using their good eyesight, they may appear to be curious and even approach us. They walk with an irregular gait but can move as fast backwards and sideways as forward. For courtship purposes, males are often strikingly marked and perform dances and wave their front legs to impress the female. At night, or in cool weather, they stay in little retreats or cocoons in hidden sites.

Egg Sac & Eggs

Egg sac is produced inside a silken nest where the female will remain on guard until the young hatch and disperse.

Diversity

About 300 species are found in North America. Ten genera in this guide.

Eris	*Hentzia*	*Phidippus*	*Sitticus*
Evarcha	*Maevia*	*Platycryptus*	
Habronattus	*Pelegrina*	*Salticus*	

Jumping Spiders (Family Salticidae)

160 Bronze Jumper (*Eris*)
161 Hoy's Jumper (*Evarcha*)
162 Agile Jumper (*Habronattus*)
163 Headdress Jumper (*Hentzia*)
164 Dimorphic Jumper (*Maevia*)
166 Reckless Jumper (*Pelegrina*)

168 Bold Jumper (*Phidippus*)
170 Distinguished Jumper (*Phidippus*)
171 Brilliant Jumper (*Phidippus*)
172 Familiar Jumper (*Platycryptus*)
173 Asian Jumper (*Sitticus*)
174 Zebra Jumper (*Salticus*)

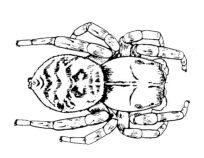

**Actual size of
adult female
Asian Jumper**

face

Bronze Jumper *Eris militaris* (female)

F
M

Common on vegetation in woodlands or their edges. Trees, shrubs and tall grasses.

Nature Notes:

Formerly known as *Eris marginata.*

May hibernate in aggregations under loose bark or in stumps.

Description: Female's body is 6 to 8 mm long. Male's is 5 to 7 mm. Legspans range from 8 to 10 mm.

Abdomen: Female has a basal white band with several pairs of oblique white spots that are partially surrounded by black patches ↑. Male has white bands edging a light gray-brown abdomen.

Carapace: Female is a lighter brown with no white bands. Male is bronze-brown with wide white side bands.

Legs: Bronze-brown with some banding.

Hunting Technique: Stalk prey on plants.

Web: None.

Egg Sac & Eggs: Egg sac is produced in summer and guarded by the female. It is usually placed under a rolled leaf.

Life Cycle: Females mature in spring and summer. Mature males can be found in nearly every month of the year. Egg sac is produced in the summer. Winter is spent as an adult or penultimate in a silken bag under loose bark or in old stumps. May hibernate in aggregations.

Hoy's Jumper *Evarcha hoyi* (male)

Meadows, fields and woodland edges. Tall grasses and bushes.

Description: Female's body is 4.5 to 6.5 mm long. Male's is 4 to 5.5 mm. Legspans range from 7 to 8.5 mm.

Abdomen: Male and female are fairly similar. A white band wraps around entire sides of abdomen except posterior tip. White chevrons on a dark background. Variable.

Carapace: Always shows a white band across the middle of the carapace and also above the anterior eyes ↑ in the ocular region.

Legs: Banded.

Hunting Technique: Pursue and pounce on prey.

Web: None.

Egg Sac & Eggs: Egg sac is produced in summer and guarded by the female.

Life Cycle: Mature in late spring and stay active until fall.

Nature Notes:

Formerly known as
Pellenes hoyi.

Agile Jumper   *Habronattus cognatus*   (male)

Along shorelines with bare sand. Under rocks and sticks.

Nature Notes:

Formerly known as *Pellenes agilis*, from which we formed the common name, Agile Jumper.

Found from New England to Florida and west to New Mexico.

Description: Female's body is 5 to 6.5 mm long. Male's is 5 to 5.5 mm. Legspans range from 7 to 8.5 mm.

Abdomen: Male shows three wide white bands (including one down the middle) ↑ and two black bands. Female is less showy with more gray and indistinct white spots.

Carapace: Male boldly patterned with four white stripes and three black ones. White band below eyes. Reddish cap ↑ is between the two rows of eyes in the ocular region.

Legs: Male has bushy hairs on leg one; used in courtship display.

Hunting Technique: Pursue and pounce on prey in sandy areas.

Web: None.

Egg Sac & Eggs: Produced in late summer.

Life Cycle: Females mature in summer. Males in late summer to fall.

Headdress Jumper   *Hentzia mitrata* (male)

Vegetation in woodlands or their edges. Common on coniferous and deciduous trees.

Description: Female's body is 4 to 5 mm long. Male's is 4 to 4.5 mm. Legspans range from 6 to 7 mm.

Abdomen: Male has white stripes down sides ↑; coppery iridescence between. Female has a median row of darker spots or chevrons on a gray-white background; small spots on side as well.

Carapace: Male has white stripes on sides; white clypeus and coppery-yellow ocular region ↑.

Legs: Very long front legs. Male's legs are all white; including first pair which also has long white hairs ↑. Female's are translucent white to yellow.

Hunting Technique: Pursue prey on plants.

Web: None.

Egg Sac & Eggs: Egg sac is placed on a branch of spruce or other suitable sites.

Life Cycle: Adult males in late spring and early summer; females throughout summer. Winter spent as penultimate instar.

Nature Notes:

Formerly known as *Icius mitratus*.

Mitrata is Latin for headdress and refers to this species coppery crown of hairs in the ocular region.

Note the white front pair of legs on the male. The color distinguishes this jumper from its cousin, *Hentzia palmarum*, the Admirable Jumper, who has black front legs.

Dimorphic Jumper *Maevia inclemens* (male; light variety)

Bushes, trees and grass. Also found under boards on the ground.

Nature Notes:

The name, Dimorphic Jumper, refers to the two forms of the male. The *niger* variety has a black body and white legs (see photo on right) while the normal lighter male is patterned with red and black chevrons on a gray body (see photo above).

Also known as *Maevia vittata*.

Description: Female's body is 7 to 10 mm long. Male's is 5 to 7 mm. Legspans range from 9 to 12 mm.

Abdomen: Female is gray with iridescent reddish side bands ↑ and grey chevrons on posterior end. Light form of male is also marked with gray, red and black but he has a narrower abdomen. Black form is entirely black.

Carapace: Female's is yellow with a dark chevron anteriorly. Male has a high cephalothorax. *Niger* male's is black with three tufts of hair on top ↑; light variety male is gray.

Legs: Yellowish in female. Whitish-gray in *niger* variety male and banded black and gray in light male. Lighter male also has striking stripes on femurs of front legs ↑.

Hunting Technique: Good eyesight allows them to approach and pounce on prey.

Mating pair of Dimorphic Jumpers. The male (on top) is the black (*niger*) variety. Compare him to the light variety male in the photo to the left. He is attempting to reach her epigynum with his palps to complete the mating process.

Web: None.

Egg Sac & Eggs: Oval mass of about sixteen eggs placed on a silk sheet. Very little silk on top of eggs. Female stands guard.

Life Cycle: Overwinters in the adult, penultimate or younger instar stage.

Reckless Jumper   *Pelegrina proterva*   (female)

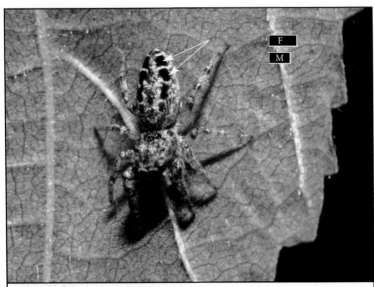

Weedy fields and nearby trees and shrubs. Meadows and woods. Often hunting on tree bark, fence posts and tall grasses. Collected by sweeping.

Nature Notes:

This species was formerly known as *Metaphidippus protervus.*

"*Proterva*" is Latin for reckless or impudent and may refer to this species bold nature.

Description: Female's body is 4 to 6 mm long. Male's is 3 to 4 mm. Legspans range from 6 to 8 mm.

Abdomen: Four pairs of squarish black spots ↑ on a tan or yellowish background. Light on front edge of abdomen. Male has broad, brown median band and an iridescent bronze abdomen with white sides ↑.

Carapace: High and convex; ocular quadrangle is two-fifths of the carapace. Rusty-brown; black in ocular area. The white along the sides is more noticeable on the males.

Legs: Yellowish with brown rings and spots. Male's legs are striped with black and white.

Body not as hairy as some jumping spiders.

Hunting Technique: Good eyesight allows them to approach and pounce on prey. They also use a dragline while hunting.

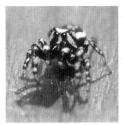

The male Reckless Jumper's face is beautifully marked with black and white stripes. Here he is looking up at the person whose hand he is sitting on.

Pelegrina proterva males are marked very differently than the females. Note his iridescent bronze body and wide white side stripes.

Web: None.

Egg Sac & Eggs: Produced in summer. They are attached to twigs and guarded by the females.

Life Cycle: Adults mature in late spring and are around until late summer. Egg sacs are produced in the summer. Spiderlings disperse rapidly. Spiders overwinter as young.

Jumping spiders, like this *Pelegrina* species, love to hunt in sunny places. Their large AME (anterior median eyes) make it look as if they are wearing tiny sunglasses. (This is not *Pelegrina proterva*).

Bold Jumper   *Phidippus audax* (female)

Very large and common jumper. Woods, gardens, tall grasses, shrubs, tree trunks, fallen limbs and leaf litter. Around and inside houses.

Nature Notes:

Members of the genus *Phidippus* are our largest jumping spiders. They have heavy, hairy bodies that are often spotted.

Young male Bold Jumpers sometimes show a red spot on the abdomen and have been mistaken for black widows.

One captive Bold Jumper ate 40 fruit flies in a single sitting!

Males court females by waving their front legs in the air.

Description: Female's body is 8 to 13 mm long. Male's is 6 to 10 mm. Legspans range from 11 to 15 mm.

Abdomen: Dark with a large red spot ↑ or white spot ↑ in the middle and two smaller white spots near the caudal end. Male is boldly marked with black and white.

Carapace: Nearly as long as the abdomen. Dark, with some white patches.

Legs: Faintly striped. Male's are black and white.

Chelicerae: Iridescent green ↑ in males.

Hunting Technique: Chase prey and pounce.

Web: None. A silken retreat is made for the eggs.

Egg Sac & Eggs: The eggs are suspended between two silk sheets and hidden in a silken retreat. The female guards them until the spiderlings disperse.

Male Bold Jumpers are boldly colored. They wave their black and white legs in front of females during courtship.

Life Cycle: Adults mature in early summer and remain active until fall. They mate in summer and later produce egg sacs. Overwinter as penultimate or younger stage. May hibernate in groups in silk sacs.

Don't let the red spot on the abdomen of this Bold Jumper fool you; it is not a black widow! Young spiders and some adults may show this red mark instead of the normal white mark.

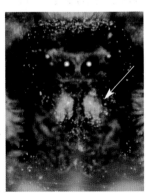

Phidippus males often have tufts of hair above the eyes and iridescent chelicerae. They swing their colorful jaws in front of the females during courtship.

Distinguished Jumper   *Phidippus princeps* (male)

Meadows, fields and woodland edges. Bushes and tall grasses.

Nature Notes:

Members of the genus *Phidippus* are our largest jumping spiders. They have heavy hairy bodies that are often spotted.

Adults of this species have been found in mud dauber wasp nests.

Description: Female's body is 9 to 13 mm long. Male's is 7 to 8 mm. Legspans range from 10 to 15 mm.

Abdomen: Male's is solid orange to brown ↑ and edged in black. Female is not as dark and has greater gray pubescence.

Carapace: Very dark brown to black in males. Females are lighter with no orange and more gray.

Legs: Hairy.

Hunting Technique: Chase prey on, over and around vegetation.

Web: None.

Egg Sac & Eggs: Egg sac is round and over a quarter-inch in diameter. It may contain over one hundred eggs. Female guards.

Life Cycle: Courtship in spring with eggs by late spring or early summer.

Brilliant Jumper *Phidippus clarus* (female)

Common species on bushes, grasses and other vegetation.

Description: Female's body is 8 to 10 mm long. Male's is 5 to 7 mm. Legspans range from 8 to 12 mm.

Abdomen: Female is mostly yellowish-orange with four pairs of white spots in thin black bands ↑. Male looks very different. Black with white band around the front of the abdomen ↑ and two side orange bands ↑. Several white spots.

Carapace: Females are grayish-black. Black in males

Legs: Yellowish-orange in females. Black in males.

Hunting Technique: Chase prey on, over and around vegetation.

Web: None.

Egg Sac & Eggs: Females guard quarter-inch egg sacs.

Life Cycle: Maturity and mating take place in early summer. Eggs later in the summer. Adults are present through the fall.

Nature Notes:

Also known as *Phidippus rimator*.

This species has been found in the mud nests of *Sceliphron* wasps (the mud dauber wasps).

The male Brilliant Jumper is very dark compared to the female. Note the beautiful orange and white bands on his abdomen.

Familiar Jumper *Platycryptus undatus*

Common under loose bark of tree trunks. Also on buildings, rocks, fences and in the leaf litter.

Nature Notes:

Form large hibernating groups of fifty or more; each in its own self-woven cocoon. They are packed in so tightly as to resemble a single silk blanket.

Formerly known as *Metacyrba undata, Marpissa undata* and *Marptusa familiaris.*

This male *P. undatus* has used its large anterior median eyes (AME) to catch a fly for dinner. Note his band of reddish hairs below the eyes in the clypeus region.

Description: Female's body is 10 to 13 mm long. Male's is 9 to 10 mm. Legspans range from 12 to 15 mm.

Abdomen: Flat and widest anteriorly. Dark with several gray chevrons near posterior end ↑. Gray pattern in middle.

Carapace: Gray and black with some longer gray hairs. Females have red eyebrow hairs and males have white. Males also show a red or brown band of hairs below the eyes ↑ (the clypeus region).

Legs: Gray and black.

Hunting Technique: Chase prey on walls, tree trunks and on the ground.

Web: None.

Egg Sac & Eggs: Summer.

Life Cycle: All ages hibernate in self-woven cocoons under logs, bark or in other protected areas. The majority are adults, though.

Asian Jumper   *Sitticus fasciger*

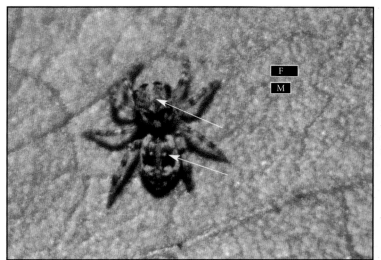

Introduced to North America from Asia. Often found in houses and other buildings.

Description: Female's body is 5 to 6 mm long. Male's is 4 to 5 mm. Legspans range from 6 to 8 mm.

Abdomen: About the same size as carapace. Central light line with pair of white spots ↑. Light waves and chevrons towards the posterior.

Carapace: Wide with rounded sides. Ocular quadrangle is about one-half the length of the carapace. Light line down center of carapace ↑. Some reddish hairs. Female is light brown with yellow markings; male is dark brown with white markings.

Legs: Annulated; Short, nearly all are same size.

Hunting Technique: Stalk and then pounce.

Web: None.

Egg Sac & Eggs: Egg sac is produced in summer. It is coated with silk and guarded by the female.

Life Cycle: Adults mature during the summer.

Nature Notes:

We wanted to include this species in the book but could not find a photo. Then, during the last week of production, this little guy hopped onto the art desk in the publishing offices. Rick corralled her while Sparky ran and got his camera. It was fate that the Asian Jumper was to be included in the book!

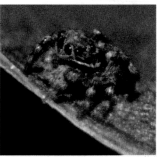

Jumping spiders always attach a silk dragline to the leaf before they leap.

Zebra Jumper *Salticus scenicus*

Unmistakable. Common on buildings, rocks, stones, trees and gardens. Many stray indoors.

Nature Notes:

I have observed them on sun-bathed walls in the early spring; probably they were hunting recently awakened flies.

I have never observed them during a North Wood's winter.

Description: Female's body is 4 to 6.5 mm long. Male's is 4 to 5.5 mm. Legspans range from 6 to 8 mm.

Abdomen: Unmistakable zebra-like black and white pattern ↑. Slightly longer than carapace. Two pairs of black and white stripes and a white band across the front of the abdomen. Males show more white striping than females.

Carapace: Longer than wide. Black with two white bands along the sides and a pair of white spots behind the posterior eyes.

Eyes: May have iridescence around the eyes.

Legs: Black and white striped.

Chelicerae: Males have very long, horizontal jaws

Hunting Technique: Like other members of this family, the Zebra Jumper actively hunts in the sunlight; locating prey with their large two front eyes (AME).

Jumping spiders can see objects over three feet away. This explains why they look up at us when we are near. They are sizing us up; is the human edible or not?

Web: None. Retreats may be constructed in crevices.

Egg Sac & Eggs: The egg sac may be placed in a hidden site such as under a stone.

Life Cycle: Mature males can be found from spring to mid summer. Females can be found from spring though the summer and into fall. Mating takes place in spring and early summer. Overwinter in the penultimate stage.

The large anterior median eyes (AME) make the jumping spider look almost comical to us. It is the human proportions on a very tiny critter that make us do a double take.

Meshweb Weavers
Family Dictynidae

Dictynids are not likely to be encountered by the casual observer, but in late summer their irregular webs can be seen in the tops of dead flowers in meadows. The webs are easy to see when covered by morning dew.

Description
Small brown spiders (3 to 5 mm). Largest family of cribellate spiders.

Abdomen: Yellow-brown or gray with dark patterns and markings.

Carapace: Yellow-brown. Long and oval.

Eyes: Two rows of four. Six eyes are light and two dark.

Legs: Short and nearly equal in length.

Chelicerae: Relatively large with teeth.

Cribellum is present.

Similar Spiders
Theridiids (cobweb weavers) make similar webs, but they are found mainly indoors. Cobweb weavers are also larger spiders with different abdomen patterns and no cribellum. Amaurobiids (hackledmesh weavers) do have a cribellum, but are larger-bodied.

Habitat
Under leaves in fields or in their webs atop dried plant stalks.

Hunting Technique
They sit and wait on the side or edge of the web. Their calamistrum is used to comb out silk from the cribellum when wrapping prey.

Web
The irregular web is constructed at the tips of plants in fields, on top of large leaves, under leaves or in crevices. Field webs are often on dead plants and best seen late in the season.

Egg Sac & Eggs
Multiple egg sacs are made by each female. The lens-shaped sacs are suspended in the web with the spider keeping watch nearby.

Diversity
About 160 species are found in North America. One genus in this guide.

Dictyna

Meshweb Weavers (Family Dictynidae)
178 Dictyna Spider species (*Dictyna*)

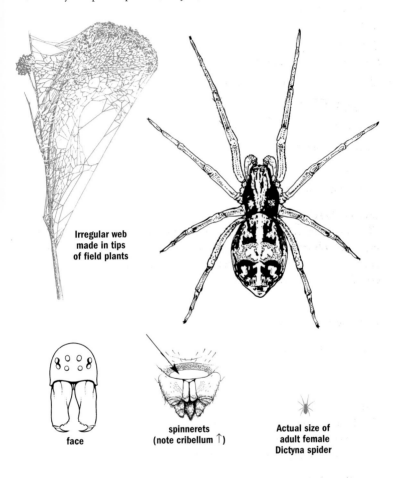

Irregular web
made in tips
of field plants

face

spinnerets
(note cribellum ↑)

Actual size of
adult female
Dictyna spider

Dictyna Spider sp. *Dictyna* species

F
M

Typically in grasslands, meadows and fields amongst the grasses and weeds. Sometimes on walls, fences and buildings. Also among dead leaves on the ground in woods.

Nature Notes:

Members of the genus *Dictyna* build irregular webs on the tops of dried flower stalks. Webs are very visible in late summer and fall. Others in this genus form webs under stones and dead leaves, on walls and fences and atop large leaves. The spider hides in the web.

It is hard to see the tiny spiders of *Dictyna*. Easiest to find may be *D. annulipes* by locating their irregular webs on the tops of plants in late summer (see photo on right hand page).

Description: Female's body is 4 mm long. Male's is 3 mm. Legspans range from 5 to 6 mm.

Abdomen: Oval. Yellowish spots in center ↑; brown on the sides. Many irregular white markings. Males are usually darker than females. The whole body is covered with fine hairs.

Carapace: Yellow in front; brown on the thoracic region.

Legs: Yellow to light brown.

Chelicerae: Male's jaws are large; they project out in front of the head and appear to be too big for such a tiny spider.

Hunting Technique: The spider hides in the web and waits.

Web: Irregular snares usually amongst the top branches and seed heads of grasses and dried weeds. Also on fences, walls and the top sides of large leaves.

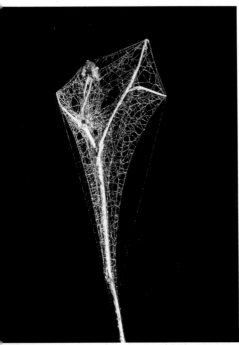

This is the irregular style of web that several *Dictyna* species construct in the tops of grasses and dried stalks. It is diagnostic of this genus.

Egg Sac & Eggs: Female may make several egg sacs and place them in the web. This occurs in summer.

Life Cycle: Spiders mature in the spring and soon mate. Egg sacs are formed in summer. Winter is spent as a penultimate or younger instar. They hibernate under loose bark or dead leaves on the ground.

Hackled Orbweavers
Family Uloboridae

Uloborids are best known as the only family of spiders in the world without venom or venom glands. The Triangle Weavers use their own bodies to anchor one corner of a triangular web.

Description
A small family of small spiders (4 to 7 mm). Some construct an orb web.

Abdomen: Brown and rounded or triangular-shaped; often with humps at the highest point of the abdomen.

Carapace: Small and brown.

Eyes: Eight. Four in two rows; may be on protuberances. All eyes are dark.

Legs: Brown. Elongated front pair with feathery growths on the tibia. Three claws.

Chelicerae: Jaws with teeth. No venom glands.

Cribellum with well developed calamistrum.

Similar Spiders
Though Araneids (orbweavers) also construct orb webs, they tend to have larger and more rounded abdomens, but some small ones may have a body similar to an Uloborid. Note, however, that orbweaver webs have sticky threads on the spirals. Hackled orbweaver webs are not sticky.

Habitat
Widespread, but not common. Bushes, shrubs and small trees.

Hunting Technique
With no poison and non-sticky webs, hackled orbweavers need to react quickly to any insect tangled in their web. Only quick reflexes allow them to catch and wrap their prey in silk to immobilize them.

Web
Hunting snares are of two types: orbs, that are horizontal, non-sticky and hackled, often with a stabilimentum; and triangular webs that are suspended vertically between twigs; the spider uses its own body to hold the third corner of the web to a twig.

Egg Sac & Eggs
Egg sac is placed in the edge of the web or on a nearby twig.

Diversity

About 15 species are found in North America. Two genera in this guide.

Hyptiotes
Uloborus

Hackled Orbweavers (Family Uloboridae)

182 Triangle Weaver (*Hyptiotes*)
183 Feather-legged Orbweaver (*Uloborus*)

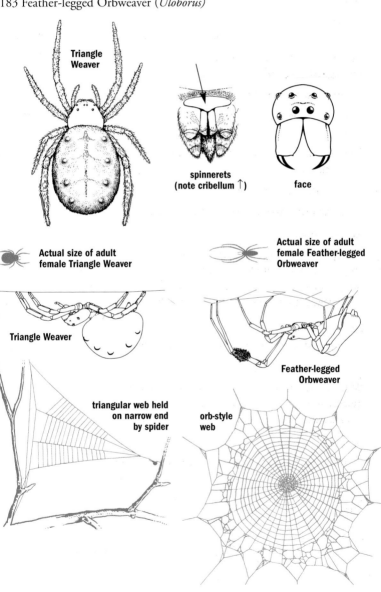

Triangle Weaver

spinnerets
(note cribellum ↑)

face

Actual size of adult
female Triangle Weaver

Actual size of adult
female Feather-legged
Orbweaver

Triangle Weaver

Feather-legged
Orbweaver

triangular web held
on narrow end
by spider

orb-style
web

Triangle Weaver   *Hyptiotes gertschi*

F
M

Deciduous forests. Underbrush and shrubs.

Nature Notes:

A tiny spider found in an almost invisible web in the shade of the summer woods. Easy to overlook.

The Triangle Weaver is a member of the family Uloboridae, the only family of spiders lacking venom of any kind.

When clinging to a branch stub and holding its web, this spider is easily mistaken for a leaf bud.

Description: Female's body is 3 to 4 mm long. Male's is 2 to 3 mm. Legspans range from 6 to 8 mm.

Abdomen: Broadly elliptical. Brownish-gray. Female with a double row of cone-shaped knobs ↑. Male has narrower and lower bumps.

Carapace: About as wide as long. Short and fairly heart-shaped. Brownish.

Eyes: Posterior lateral eyes (PLE) are far to the side of the other eyes.

Legs: Short and stout.

Pedipalps: Male's are large and projecting.

Hunting Technique: The spider attaches itself to a twig with silk and holds the web with its first legs; making the spider itself, part of the web. When an insect gets caught, the spider pulls the web taut, then slackens it to snare the victim.

Web: A triangular orb with four radii. The web appears to be a partially completed orb web. Threads are hackled and non-sticky.

Egg Sac & Eggs: Formed in late summer.

Life Cycle: They mature in summer. Egg sacs are formed in late summer. Overwinter as eggs.

Feather-legged Orbweaver *Uloborus glomosus*

Well-shaded woods. Bushes or low branches of trees.

Description: Female's body is 3 to 5 mm long. Male's is 2 to 3 mm. Legspans range from 6 to 10 mm.

Abdomen: Triangular with a pair of dorsal humps ↑ about one-third of the distance from the anterior end on the female. Male has a flat abdomen with no humps.

Carapace: Oval with no humps. Brownish.

Legs: First pair of legs is much longer and more stout than the other pairs. These legs may be four-times the length of the carapace. Tibia of leg number one on the female has a cluster of hairs at the distal end.

Hunting Technique: Due to non-sticky webs, only quick reflexes allow them to catch and wrap their prey in silk to immobilize them.

Web: A small web; only four to six inches in diameter. Often horizontal and made of non-sticky threads. Spirals are made of hackled threads. May have stabilimentum or sheeted hub.

Egg Sac & Eggs: Eggs formed in the summer. The egg sac is suspended at the side of the web.

Life Cycle: Mature in spring. Eggs in the summer. Winter is spent as a half-grown immature.

Nature Notes:

The family Uloboridae is the only family of spiders in the world with no poison glands.

Hackledmesh Weavers
Family Amaurobiidae

Not often seen. Amaurobiids are probably best known by their huge carapace that is actually larger than their abdomen.

Description
Medium-sized spiders (5 to 9 mm). Robust. Brown or black. Largest of the cribellates.

Abdomen: Rounded. Black or brown with patterns.

Carapace: Long, robust and nearly as long as the abdomen. Brown or black.

Eyes: Two rows; nearly all equally-sized and colored. Anterior lateral eyes (ALE) and posterior lateral eyes (PLE) nearly touch.

Legs: Stout and somewhat spiny.

Chelicerae: Powerful; with teeth.

Cribellum in two parts.

Similar Spiders
Agelenids (funnel weavers) make a web that also may have a tubular retreat, but they have different carapaces and long spinnerets. Lycosids (wolf spiders) have large posterior median eyes (PME).

Habitat
They live under bark, in cracks and amongst rock piles.

Hunting Technique
They hunt at night from their web.

Web
Hunting snare is an irregular loose web with coarse hackling and a tubular retreat. Constructed on walls, trees and among the leaf litter.

Observations
Males court females by drumming on the web with their palps. Reach maturity in autumn.

Egg Sac & Eggs: Egg sac is flattened, spherical and whitish. Attached to the web.

Diversity
About 80 species are found in North America. One genus in this guide.

Callobius (Amaurobius)

Hackledmesh Weavers (Family Amaurobiidae)
186 Bennett's Hackledmesh Weaver (*Callobius*)

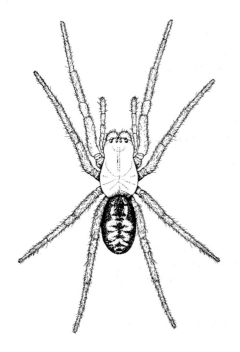

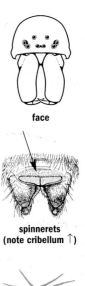

face

spinnerets
(note cribellum ↑)

Actual size of
adult female
Bennett's
Hackledmesh Weaver

Bennett's Hackledmesh Weaver *Callobius bennetti*

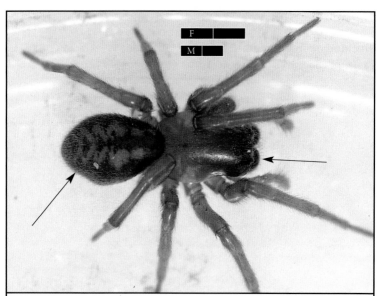

Forest leaf litter. Under logs and stones.

Nature Notes:

Formerly known as *Amaurobius bennetti*.

Members of the Amaurobiidae can be confused with wolf spiders when they are seen amongst the leaf litter. Wolf spiders, though, do not make webs and have much larger eyes.

Amaurobids have carapaces that are as large, or larger, than their abdomens.

Description: Female's body is 5 to 9 mm long. Male's is 5 to 7 mm. Legspans range from 12 to 18 mm.

Abdomen: Ovoid. Brown with two yellowish median bands and three pale chevrons at posterior end ↑.

Carapace: Robust and brown ↑. Wider than the abdomen and nearly as long.

Legs: Brownish-yellow. Fairly long and strong. Calamistrum is less than one-third that of the metatarsus number four.

Chelicerae: Cheliceral fangs have four teeth.

Hunting Technique: They hunt at night from their web.

Web: A loose irregular sheet web with coarse hackling.

Egg Sac & Eggs: Egg sacs are formed in late summer or fall.

Life Cycle: Mature in spring. Egg sacs are formed in late summer or fall. Winter is spent as an immature.

Spitting Spiders
Family Scytodidae

Spitting spiders are best known for their spitting! Viscous silk tangles prey and secures the victim to the ground. May be encountered on buildings as they hunt.

Description
Medium-sized spiders (6 to 10mm). Carapace and abdomen are nearly equal in size. Most are yellow with black spots. Large venom glands.

Abdomen: Rounded and only slightly larger than the carapace. Yellow with black spots.

Carapace: Rounded, as seen from above; high and domed, as seen from the side. Like the abdomen, the carapace is yellow with black spots and markings.

Eyes: Six in three pairs of two.

Legs: All legs nearly equal in length. Legs are yellow and ringed with black.

Similar Spiders
May superficially resemble some Theridiids (cobweb weavers) which build webs in which they hang upside down. Spitting spiders do not build webs. Cobweb weavers have eight eyes compared to the six of spitting spiders.

Habitat
On buildings and rocks. When in buildings, they are seen in shaded corners and dark closets. Members of this family are most common in the tropics.

Hunting Technique
Since they are slow spiders who don't build a web, they must use another trick to capture prey. Venom and sticky threads are spit out from the spider onto the victim. The threads are sprayed in a fast back-and-forth pattern that not only captures the prey but attaches it to the substrate.

Web
Does not build hunting snares or any other webs.

Observations
Spitting spiders spit sticky threads up to three quarters of an inch (two centimeters). These threads anchor the victim in place, allowing them to administer the fatal bite. They hide during the day.

Egg Sac & Eggs
The egg sac is held by the female in her jaws.

Diversity

About 10 species are found in North America. One genus in this guide.

Scytodes

Spitting Spiders (Family Scytodidae)

190 Spitting Spider (*Scytodes*)

carapace viewed
from the side

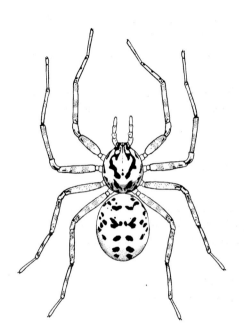

face

Actual size of
adult female
Spitting Spider

Spitting Spider *Scytodes thoracica*

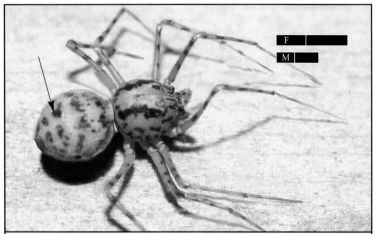

F |
M |

Often on walls of buildings; outside and inside. May be seen in cellars, dark corners, closets, etc. Rocky areas.

Nature Notes:

Venom and sticky threads are spit out from the spider onto the prey. The threads are sprayed in a fast back-and-forth pattern that not only captures the prey but attaches it to the substrate.

The only spider in the region that uses this method to catch prey. I have observed them hunting during the day on the walls of buildings.

Found at the southern edge of the North Woods.

Description: Female's body is 5 to 8 mm long. Male's is 4 to 5 mm long. Legspans range from 12 to 20 mm.

Abdomen: Quite rounded. Slightly larger than the carapace. Yellow with several rows of dark spots ↑. The front ones are nearly joined to form bands.

Carapace: Oval and high to contain the large sticky-gum-producing glands. Yellow with black markings.

Legs: Same color as the body; yellow with brown rings.

Hunting Technique: Venom and sticky threads are spit out from the spider onto the prey. The threads are sprayed in a fast back-and-forth pattern that not only captures the prey but attaches it to the substrate.

Web: None.

Egg Sac & Eggs: Produced in late summer. It is held by the female until the spiderlings hatch.

Life Cycle: Matures in early summer. After mating in late summer, the egg sac is produced. Probably overwinters as an immature, but some adults may live more than a year.

Poisonous Spiders in the North Woods?

Nearly all spiders have poison glands, and so technically, nearly all spiders are poisonous. But the question is "poisonous to whom"? The venom injected into insect prey is intended to kill them quickly. But what effect does this venom have on humans? For the most part, none. The two spiders included in this book that have venom strong enough to harm man are the Northern Widow (*Latrodectus variolus*) and the Brown Recluse (*Loxosceles reclusa*). Neither is native to the North Woods and rarely, if ever, seen. The handful of records of these species are of spiders that were most likely transported north, usually to a single house. There are no known colonies of either spider in our region.

Out-of-towner; the Northern Widow is rarely seen in the North Woods.

Furthermore, what is often thought to be a "spider bite" is usually not. Some authorities believe that 80 percent or more of alleged bites from spiders are likely those of insects. If a spider does bite, it is in self-defense when we accidentally press against it. Spiders do not seek out humans! Allergies and other skin reactions are no doubt possible, but these are due to the person's body chemistry and not the spider's venom. Though we have all heard of danger-ous or painful bites, they are usually in other parts of the country, or world, and many are not reliable stories to begin with. We are much more likely to get bit by our own pet than by a spider. Spiders get a bum rap in the danger department.

Another foreigner; the Brown Recluse.

Brown Recluse *Loxosceles reclusa* (Family Sicariidae)

Often indoors; usually hidden behind furniture or other dark areas. Under boards, stones and log piles outdoors. An exotic species that is naturalized in southern states.

Nature Notes:

Brown Recluses are not aggressive, but they have been known to bite if disturbed. The wound develops a crust and a surrounding red zone. The crust falls off, leaving a deep crater, which often does not heal for months.

Not know to exist in the North Woods unless carried here from locations further south.

Only one record from northern Minnesota: a Lake County home in 1953.

Description: Female's body is 9 to 12 mm long. Male's is 6 to 8 mm. Legspans range from 25 to 35 mm.

Abdomen: Grayish to dark brown with no obvious patterns.

Carapace: Flat. Yellow-brown with a dark violin-shape ↑ on dorsum. Base of "violin" at the head end.

Eyes: Six eyes in three pairs ↑.

Legs: All legs are long and thin. First pair is more than four times as long as the carapace.

Hunting Technique: Web hunter. Only bites when disturbed.

Web: Loose, irregular strands constructed under bark and stones.

Egg Sac & Eggs: A single female may produce up to five egg sacs.

Life Cycle: Spiders mature in spring and mate throughout the summer. Young take nearly a year to develop. Overwinter as immatures.

Northern Widow   *Latrodectus variolus* (Family Theridiidae)

F

M

Undisturbed woods and grasslands. Stumps, under logs, stones, stone walls and entrances to abandoned animal burrows. May be among bushes and trees in dry regions.

Description: Female's body is 9 to 11 mm. Male's is 5 to 6 mm. Legspans range from 15 to 30 mm.

Abdomen: Globular and shiny. Black with red spots ↑ down center of dorsum. Red "hour glass" under the belly is in two parts ↑; not joined in the middle (see photo lower right). Male is smaller with four white bands on sides of a thin abdomen.

Carapace: Small and black.

Legs: Thin, black and hairy.

Hunting Technique: Web hunter. Only bites when disturbed.

Web: A horizontal sheet that has many irregular vertical threads extended from it and a funnel-like retreat. Webs placed under stones, logs and abandoned animal burrows.

Egg Sac & Eggs: Egg sacs are pear-shaped; pale gray, tan or yellow. They are placed in the web and guarded by the female.

Life Cycle: Adults mature in the spring and then mate. Spiders overwinter as adults or in the penultimate stage.

Nature Notes:

Venom of the Northern Widow may be as potent as the Southern Black Widow's, but these spiders are timid and non-aggressive. The bite is not particularly painful and may go unnoticed. An hour later strong abdominal cramps develop. The pain and cramping can effect breathing. Lethal in less than one percent of cases.

Very rare in the North Woods. Has been recorded in the northern part of lower Michigan.

Males may be killed and eaten by females.

Glossary

Abdomen: The posterior portion of a spider body.

ALE: Anterior lateral eyes.

AME: Anterior median eyes.

Anal Tubercle: Small projection at the posterior end of the abdomen on which the anus opens.

Annulated: Showing rings of pigmentation, as on a leg. Ringed or banded.

Anterior: Toward the front.

Appendages: Structures extending away from the body proper; for example, legs, palps, etc.

Arachnida: Class in the phylum Arthropoda that includes spiders, harvestmen, ticks, mites, scorpions, whipscorpions, windscorpions and pseudoscorpions.

Arachnology: The scientific study of arachnids (including spiders).

Araneae: The arachnid order of spiders.

Araneologist: A biologist who specializes in the study of spiders.

Araneomorphae: One of the two infraorders of spiders (the other is Mygalomorphae). Most true spiders are in this group

Book lung: A respiratory organ with page-like folds that is found in most spiders.

Calamistrum: A series of curved bristles on the fourth leg of some spiders (cribellate spiders). Used to comb out silk threads for prey capture.

Carapace: Top of the cephalothorax. The fused series of sclerites making up the dorsal part of the cephalothorax.

Caudal: The posterior end.

Cephalothorax: The anterior of the two major divisions into which the body of a spider is divided. It is the head and thorax combined.

Cervical groove: The furrow which extends forward and toward the sides from the center of the carapace and marks the boundary between the head and the thorax. It is sometimes indistinct or completely lacking.

Chelicerae: The jaws; consisting of a pair of stout basal segments each with a terminal fang.

Claw: A strong curved process at the distal end of the leg.

Claw tufts: The bunch of hairs at the tip of the tarsus in those spiders with only two claws.

Clypeus: The region or the cephalothorax between the anterior eyes and the chelicerae.

Comb: Bristles with barbs on tarsus 4 in members of the family Theridiidae. Used to "comb out" silk onto prey.

Coxa: The segment of the leg (or pedipalp) nearest the body.

Cribellate: Adjective referring to a spider that possesses a cribellum.

Cribellum: A silk-spinning, transverse, plate-like organ in front of the spinnerets in cribellate spiders. It produces the hackled band silk threads.

Denticle: A small, smooth tooth, usually on chelicerae, legs or palps.

Distal: At the opposite end of the point of attachment.

Dorsal: Situated near the top or above other sections.

Dorsal Furrow: A median groove, depression or pigmented line behind the cervical groove on the carapace.

Dorsum: The back, or upper surface, of the spider.

Ecribellate: Adjective referring to a spider that does not possess a cribellum.

Egg Sac: Spider eggs enclosed in a silk casing.

Endite: One of the mouth parts; ventral to the mouth opening and lateral to the lip, so that in chewing it opposes the chelicerae.

Entomophagous: Feeding on insects. Spiders are entomophagous.

Exuviae: The cast off "skin" of a molting spider. The old exoskeleton of an arthropod.

Fangs: Claw-like segments on the spider's chelicerae. Used to inject poison.

Femur: The third segment of the pedipalp or leg, counting from nearest the body.

Folium: Pigmented pattern on the abdomen, often shaped like an oak leaf. Common in the Araneidae orbweavers.

Hub: Central area of a web; as in an orb web where the radial threads converge.

Immature: A non-adult spider.

Instar: The stage of the immature spider between successive molts.

Kleptoparasite: A spider that steals prey caught by another spider.

Labium: The lower lip between the two endites of spiders.

Laterigrade: A sideways type of locomotion; as in the crab spiders and their allies. Also, the way the legs are turned in on these spiders so that the dorsal surface is posterior.

Lung Slits: External openings to the book lungs; located along the epigastric furrow.

Metatarsus: The sixth segment of the leg or pedipalp, counting from nearest the body.

Mygalimorphae: One of the two infraorders of spiders (the other is Mygalomorphae). Members include the tarantulas and trap-door spiders.

Ocular Quadrangle: The area on the carapace enclosed by the two rows of eyes.

Opisthosoma: The posterior body region of a spider. Another name for the abdomen.

Orb: A web consisting of radial strands on which spiral or circular threads are arranged in a single plane. The stereotypical spider web.

Palp: The segments of the pedipalp distal to the endite or coxa. In females it resembles a leg; in males it is modified for sperm transfer.

Patella: The fourth segment of the leg or pedipalp, counting from nearest the body.

Pedicel: The small stalk connecting the abdomen to the cephalothorax.

Pedipalp: The second appendage of the cephalothorax, behind the chelicerae but in front of the legs. They are tipped with the palp bulb.

PLE: Posterior lateral eyes.

PME: Posterior median eyes.

Posterior: Rear end; or toward the rear.

Prosoma: The anterior body region of a spider. Another name for the cephalothorax.

Proximal: The point of attachment of an appendage; or toward it.

Recurved: A curved arc such that the ends are nearer to the posterior of the body than its center.

Retromargin: The margin of the cheliceral fang furrow farther from the front of the body, nearer the endite.

Scopula: A brush of hairs on the lower surface of the tarsus and metatarsus in some spiders.

Scutum: A sclerotized plate; as on the abdomen of some spiders.

Spinnerets: The silk-spinning, paired appendages on the end of the abdomen. There are six.

Spinose: Provided with spines.

Spiracle: The opening of the tubular tracheae on the ventral side of the abdomen.

Spur: A cuticular process; heavier than a spine.

Spurious Claws: The serrated bristles at the end of the tarsus.

Stabilimentum: The bands of silk spun by certain orb-weavers in webs; often zigzag.

Sternum: The central plate on the underside of the cephalothorax of a spider.

Tarsus: The last segment of the leg or pedipalp, counting from nearest the body.

Thorax: That portion of the cephalothorax posterior to the cervical groove.

Tibia: The fifth segment of the leg or pedipalp, counting from nearest the body.

Tracheae: Tubes through which air is carried inside the body of the spider and which open at the spiracle.

Trichobothria: A fine sensory hair protruding at a right angle from the leg.

Trochanter: The second segment of the leg or pedipalp, counting from nearest the body.

Tubercle: A low, usually rounded, process.

Venter: The underside of the spider.

Ventral: Situated underneath or below other sections.

Appendix A
Titles of Interest

Dondale, C.D. and J.H. Redner. 1978, 82, 90, 92. *The Insects and Arachnids of Canada; Parts 5, 9, 17, 19.* Ottawa, ON, Canada: Department of Agriculture.

Foelix, R.F. 1996. *Biology of Spiders.* New York, NY: Oxford University Press.

Gertsch, W.J. 1979 (1949). *American Spiders.* New York, NY: VanNostrand-Reinhold.

Hillyard, P. 1994. *The Book of the Spider: A Compendium of Arachno-facts and Eight-legged Lore.* New York, NY: Avon Books.

Jackman, J.A. 1997. *A Field Guide to Spiders and Scorpions of Texas.* Houston, TX: Gulf Publishing Company.

Jones, D. 1983. *The Larousse Guide to Spiders.* New York, NY: Larouse Company. (A guide to spiders of Europe)

Kaston, B.J. 1978. *How to Know the Spiders.* Dubuque, IA: Wm. C. Brown Company.

Kaston, B.J. 1981. *Spiders of Connecticut.* Revised ed. Bull. 70. State Geological and Natural History Survey of Connecticut.

Levi, H. W. and L. R. Levi. 1996 (1968). *Spiders and Their Kin.* New York, NY: Golden Press.

Milne, L. and M. Milne. 1998. *National Audubon Society Field Guide to North American Insects and Spiders.* New York, NY: Alfred A. Knopf.

Moulder, B. 1992. *A Guide to the Common Spiders of Illinois.* Springfield, IL: Illinois State Museum.

Preston-Mafham, K. 1998. *Identifying Spiders.* Edison, NJ: Quintet Books.

Preston-Mafham, R. 1991. *The Book of Spiders and Scorpions.* New York, NY: Crescent Books.

Preston-Mafham, R. and K. Preston-Mafham. 1984. *Spiders of the World.* New York, NY: Facts On File Publications.

Shaw, J. 1987. *John Shaw's Closeups in Nature.* New York, NY: Amphoto.

Weber, L. 1996. *Backyard Almanac.* Duluth, MN: Pfeifer-Hamilton Publishers.

West, L. 1994. *How to Photograph Insects and Spiders.* Mechanicsburg, PA: Stackpole Books.

Appendix B
Additional References

Breene, R.G. 1995. *Common Names of Arachnids.* 1995. South Padre Island, TX: The American Tarantula Society.

Cutler, B. 1973. *Synanthropic Spiders: Araneae of the Twin Cities Area.* The Minnesota Academy of Science. 39: 38-39.

Cutler, B., Grim, L.H. and H.M. Kulman. 1975. *A Study in the Summer Phenology of Dionychious Spiders from Northern Minnesota Forests.* Great Lakes Entomologist. 8: 99-104.

Guarisco, H., Cutler, B. and K.E. Kinnman. 2001. *Checklist of Kansas Jumping Spiders.* Kansas School Naturalist; Emporia State University.

Heimer, S., Nentwig, W. and B. Cutler. 1984. *The Spider Fauna of Itasca State Park.* Faunistische Abhandlungen 11: 119-124.

Jass, J.P. 1995. *Life Cycle Patterns in Wisconsin Spiders.* Field Station Bulletin. Milwaukee Museum.

Jennings, D.T. and B. Cutler. 1996. *Crab Spiders of Ramsey County, Minnesota.* Gen. Tech. Rep. NC-185. St. Paul, MN.

Levi, H.W. and H.M. Field. 1954. *The Spiders of Wisconsin.* American Midland Naturalist. 51: 440-467.

Levi, H.W., Levi, L.R. and J.L. Kaspar 1958. *Harvestmen and Spiders of Wisconsin; Additional Species and Notes.* Wisconsin Academy of Science. 47: 43-52.

Roth, V. 1985. *Spider Genera of North America.* American Arachnology Society.

Snider, R.J. 1991. *A Preliminary List of the Spiders of Michigan.* Michigan Academician. 24: 201-246.

Appendix C
Spider Conservation Groups and Websites

American Arachnological Society
American Museum of Natural History
Central Park West at 79th St.
New York, NY 10024

Jumping Spiders of America North of Mexico
http://spiders.arizona.edu/salticidae/na.salticidae.html
Dr. Wayne Maddison is a jumping spider specialist. Many photographs.

International Society of Arachnology
http://160.111.87.78/ISA/default.html
An international organization website with abstracts of scientific papers.

World Spider Catalog
http://research.amnh.org/entemology/spiders/catalog81-87/index.html
American Museum of Natural History site with updated nomenclature and classification of the world's spiders.

Appendix D
Photo Credits

All photographs in this book, except the ones listed below, were taken by the author.

David Liebman: pages 169 (top), 192 (top).

Rod Planck: cover (top), pages 17 (top), 161, 162, 164, 165, 172 (bottom).

Sparky Stensaas: pages 1 (top & bottom), 8, 9 (top), 10 (bottom), 12 (top), 26 (bottom), 27 (bottom), 28, 44, 45 (bottom), 49, 56, 69 (top), 70, 71, 72, 93 (top), 97 (top), 99 (top), 105 (top), 125 (bottom), 154, 167 (top & middle), 173 (top & bottom), 175 (top & bottom).

Larry West: pages 53 (bottom), 54, 107 (top), 117 (top), 147 (middle), 149, 163, 167 (bottom), 178.

CBS Inc: pages 1 (middle right), 183.

Index